SUCCESSFUL COACHING LESSONS
—— BY AN ——
OLD SCHOOL COACH

RON MAYBERRY

Copyright © 2023 Ron Mayberry.

All rights reserved. No part of this book may be reproduced, stored, or transmitted by any means—whether auditory, graphic, mechanical, or electronic—without written permission of both publisher and author, except in the case of brief excerpts used in critical articles and reviews. Unauthorized reproduction of any part of this work is illegal and is punishable by law.

ISBN: 978-1-63950-204-2 (sc)
ISBN: 978-1-63950-205-9 (e)

This publication contains the opinions and ideas of its author. It is intended to provide helpful and informative material on the subjects addressed in the publication. The author and publisher specifically disclaim all responsibility for any liability, loss, or risk, personal or otherwise, which is incurred as a consequence, directly or indirectly, of the use and application of any of the contents of this book.

Writers Apex

Gateway Towards Success

8063 MADISON AVE #1252
Indianapolis, IN 46227
+13176596889
www.writersapex.com

INTRODUCTION

Why would anyone want to read this book. Good question, that demands an answer. Everyone is a coach in some manner or another. It does not matter what you are doing, someone is going to tell you how to do whatever you are doing. That is coaching in the most important form that exists. Plumbers are coached, cooks are coached, repairmen are coached, children are coached [most of the time by parents], barbers are coached, the President of the United States is coached, doctors are coached, policemen are coached, and the list can go on and on. As far as I am concerned, I have not won any national championships, nor have I been in demand for speaking engagements. If you compare my coaching record to others, my won loss record is good, but it does not stand out. With that said, let me explaned what I have to offer then you decide. This book is not just about my life as a coach but rather, the lessons I have learned through my coaching career. "Old School" is about coaching period. It is not a particular sport, gender, age, or level of play. I have coached on every level of play that exists in schools, coached both genders on those levels along with almost every sport that a school offers. Everyone coaches sometime in their lifetime. It doesn't have to be about a sport, and could be many things. Since I ended up with over 1000 wins coaching basketball at thirty-one different schools along with twenty-six different Head basketball coaching positions without a losing record, I guess you could say my main sport was basketball. At this point in time, I know of no one in the United States of America that can match that record nor do I know anyone wants to top me. But what clearly defines me as a basketball coach is my success rate of taking a basketball program that is on hard times and turning it into a winner. **<u>Successful Coaching lessons by an Old School Coach</u>** covers the lessons I have learned in coaching. My assistant football coaching record **of 142-43** tells you the quality of the Head coaches I worked with in football and I owe so much of my success to them. However, I enjoyed equally well coaching golf, track, tennis, cross- country and volleyball in both genders. The bottom line with my story is what I have learned in my fifty-three years of coaching. From the start of my career to the end of my career, I have provided coachable lessons in each chapter. There are **170** coaching lessons in **<u>Successful Coaching Lessons by an Old School Coach.</u>**

No doubt I have a strong passion for coaching and a passion for sports, particularly competitive sports. **I believe that athletics is a huge part of the educational process. I believe that athletics is the best example we have in the educational process where discipline, commitment and teamwork are expected of the students. When these attributes are applied elsewhere in education, all student's success rate improves.** Another reason I write this book is for the common coach that coaches any sport, not just basketball. The common coach is the majority in the real world of coaching. That includes people coaching only to help someone to learn a trade or a job. Only about 4% of coaches live in that glass house of big money and big fame. The common coach in schools across the world is where the work is done from the early morning hour till the sun goes down. The hours are long, and the pay isn't exciting. Coaches at schools deal with unhappy and happy parents, administrators, and faculty**, but more important, they deal with our youth of today**. The common coach in schools has more influence on our youth of today than anyone except parents. They live in the real world of coaching and I have a great amount of respect for the job they do. Any success I had as a coach is directly related to my background, my experiences, and the coaches I coached against, and most important, the players that played under my leadership. Thanks, and hope you enjoy the book.

ABOUT THE AUTHOR

Ron is the author of five non-fiction books called, Teachable Moments for all Educators; The Journey of a Yellow Bird; Fun Fundamental Basketball; Principles of Successful Coaching by an Old School Coach; Least We Forget, High School Coaching Legends from the Texas Panhandle and Plains Region, and a fiction book called Education 101, One Man's Journey to the Final Four. This book is a revision of Principles of Successful Coaching by an Old School Coach. He decided that content and structure needed improvement so he changed the format of the book and the title of the book.

He wrote and developed a golf magazine called "Midland College Golf" and has been a sports guest columnist twice for the Carlsbad, New Mexico City newspaper called the Current-Argus.

In the coaching world, he has over 1000 total wins to his credit, being the Head Basketball Coach at twenty-one different high schools without a losing record. He has been inducted into three Hall of Fames, coached seventeen basketball players that have played professional basketball, six All-Americans. He was the CEO of a college basketball recruiting service called "Who's Who in Juco". He was selected by the Texas Association of Basketball Coaches [the largest in the world] as the State "Coach of the Year" three times and runner-up once. He was also selected by Basketball Times Magazine as the "National Junior College Coach" in the spring of 1992. In 1982, he was selected as the keynote speaker of the National NAIA Basketball Tournament, and he has conducted basketball camps and clinics throughout the United States, the Canary Islands, and Venezuela.

CONTENTS

CHAPTER ONE..1

    a. Grace
    b. Coaching must be surrounded by love and compassion
    c. Peer learning
    d. Putting labels on students
    e. Finding out what gives your athlete a swagger
    f. Leading by example
    g. To relate you must open your mind
    h. Play to win/have a plan
    i. Search/seek different ways to reach out
    j. Boys mature late
    k. How to cut players from a team
    l. Real coaching is unselfish actions
    m. Evaluation is coaching
    n. It's not what you do but how you do it
    o. Letting players be players
    p. What makes a great athletic parent?
    q. Learn to communicate
    r. What makes a great teacher/coach?
    s. Making demands that conflict with parents

CHAPTER TWO 16

    a. Favoritism is never a secret
    b. Why take it out on an athlete-just because you **DO NOT LIKE ATHLETICS**

    c. Actions speak louder than words
    d. Egotistical coaches forget what coaching is about
    e. There is always a higher level of play-you just **JUST DON'T KNOW IT**
    f. Forget the past-look to the future-teach and coach the present
    g. A coach inspires their players to do better
    h. A coach needs a philosophy concerning injuries
    i. Stay humble if you want to coach different cultures
    j. When players feel they have no chance you have failed
    k. Coaches need to be aware of negative verbal comments
    l. Do you have a passion for being a coach?
    m. You must learn to listen if you want to be a good coach
    n. Coaches must find a way to motivate just like you were motivated
    o. You must be smarter than the equipment you use
    p. Don't burn bridges if you want to be successful

CHAPTER THREE..31

    a. Coaches need to work at teaching just like they **DO COACHING**
    b. Leaders are in control and you know it
    c. A coach is expected to be a positive leader
    d. Professionalism is the backbone in the educational system
    e. Mentoring needs to be honest and to the point
    f. How to interview for a coaching position
    g. A coach is hired to do the job/not question the job
    h. There is no substitute for enthusiasm in a coach
    i. When challenged-don't get defensive-stay in control and be humble
    j. Home- visits-the real deal if you can do it

k. A coach must understand community needs to be successful
l. Learning watching six on six girls' basketball
m. The coaching fraternity is there to help you-if you ask
n. Small -school vs. large school
o. The ultimate reward for a coach

CHAPTER FOUR 45

a. The greatest lesson a coach can learn
b. Competition done right can be motivation for IMPROVEMENT
c. Every coach needs a mentor
d. A coach needs to learn how to take care of facilities
e. All coaches can learn from each other
f. It doesn't matter what you know but rather what you can coach
g. Respect must be demanded in the coaching arena
h. Eat your pride - find the right time-confrontation
i. Coaches need to learn how to adapt to there players
j. The key to winning is good leadership
k. Coaches must step up to the plate and do there job
l. The greatest teacher for you is your opponent
m. Don't wait-an administrative certificate is a must
n. Professional courtesy is part of professionalism
o. You don't have to like all of your players but you need to love all of them

CHAPTER FIVE 58

a. Be who you are and not someone else when you coach
b. Stay on track with what you know if you want
c. Teach and coach to your strengths-stay away from your **Weaknesses**

- d. Everyone is always looking for a coach that can can do the job
- e. Talking the talk then walking the walk creates a team atmosphere
- f. What makes for great leadership at the top
- g. What a championship program looks like
- h. Never forget why you were hired
- i. Some players need a strong push in order to be effective
- j. Sharing athletes in high school—one big issue
- k. All coaching positions have job descriptions that are not written
- l. If you coach your spouse is critical for your success-they need to be a trooper
- m. How to coach your own blood?
- n. Don't baby your best player-it has to be real-not a fake job
- o. Never lose perspective about winning

CHAPTER SIX 71

- a. Who are you learning from?
- b. The survival of the fittest
- c. Playing hard vs. playing soft
- d. No dynasty without strong administrative support
- e. Community support is the bottom line for success on the high school level
- f. What makes "Friday Night Lights" special for the basketball program?
- g. How about adapting your program to the players on board
- h. Are you keeping up with the game you are coaching?
- i. Coaching is a two - way street and it starts with you
- j. Tough decisions need to be made based on what is right for your team from the best player to the worst
- k. Jealousy between coaches in different sports never has a good ending

l. A good coach learns to listen to their spouse because they will tell you the truth whether you like it or not
m. Expectations are the key to success and failure
n. Good-things happen when you stay the course and finish the job
o. Think seriously before you jump into coaching on the college-level
p. Never get satisfied with your recruiting in college
q Don't stay a home-boy all your life-expand your knowledge and experience
r. Every coach needs to have a plan concerning how officials

CHAPTER SEVEN 86

a. If you want to learn-ask and you will receive
b. How to change a program attitude
c. Style of play
d. Everyone deserves the opportunity to fail
e. Be aggressive when you get the chance but **REMAIN HUMBLE**
f. Don't judge a book by its cover
g. If you say it –you better do it
h. Know your style in recruiting and stick with it
i. It's all in how you think
j. Playing not to get beat
k. It's impossible for a problem to be solved by the same people that created the problem
l. Always give yourself twenty-four hours before you respond to an emotional situation that is stressful
m. Winning at Wayland
n. Making history is hard but worth the effort

- o. Professionalism is a two -way street
- p. Don't mess with chemistry
- q. Who's in charge?
- r. What every college coach must face sooner or later
- s. Why drug test in college
- t. Stick to your guns, stay the course
- w. Be loyal to your commitment

CHAPTER EIGHT..101

- a. A president with character
- b. Standing up for what is right for all concerned
- c. Have you already made your mind up about that **PLAYER?**
- d. When it comes to discipline-treat your players like family
- e. How to stop a team from self- destruction
- f. A good administrator projects support and confidence
- g. Do you know technique?
- h. Number one rule-make time for your family
- i. How do you counter cheating in college athletics?
- j. Character is doing what is right even when everyone thinks what you did was wrong
- k. Be prepared for the unexpected in recruiting
- l. It's one thing to get to the top but another to stay at the top
- m. Too much attention destroys some athletes
- n. Chemistry is the answer if you can understand it
- o. The Burger King Miracle-chemistry can be luck
- p. The strongest factor in winning is the commitment to the team
- q Poor administrator vs. excellent administrator
- r. Winning-what is winning

CHAPTER NINE **117**

    a.   It takes a family to change an attitude
    b.   Are you using the talent God gave you?
    c.   Join the fraternity for coaches that benefit **COACHES**
    d.   There are many ways to skin a cat
    e.   One of the great joys of coaching-staying in touch
    f.   **GOOD** teachers make the world go around in a **BETTER WAY**
    g.   When you do your job and do it right, good things happen that you can't explain
    h.   The difference between coaching men and women
    i.   Does anyone appreciate the job you are doing?
    j.   The difference between coaching basketball in New Mexico and Texas
    l.   What separates administrators?
    m.   If you want support for your program-give give support to other programs
    n.   Never-never assume anything in the educational arena
    o.   It is very hard to understand something that a a players can't see
    p.   What comes around goes around
    q.   You want to know why your team wins. Why you lose-Watch your practice

CHAPTER TEN **126**

    a.   How to make the best of a terrible coaching job
    b.   Think twice before you open your mouth- **ESPECIALLY WHEN** you are in the spotlight
    c.   Fifth season of participation
    d.   Environment has a lot to do with the way officials officiate basketball

e. Good- administration works best when they cover for the weakness and strength of each other
f. If you want a change- it must start with you- then you must lead and be patient
g. A good mentor knows when it is time to step up to the plate
h. Work ethic is something that you can't fake
i. Old saying but true-you want a successful start at the middle school-that is the life blood of of your program
j. It's never too late to learn-and if you will listen you can learn from someone that you never thought you could
k. It takes two to tango
l. How do you beat someone you aren't supposed to beat

SCHOOLS I HAVE WORKED FOR

Northside High School / 6A/ FT. Worth, Texas [Student teaching, assistant boys' basketball coach]

Perryton Junior High School/ 3A/Perryton, Texas [Teacher-Math and P.E.]

Adrian High School/ 1A/Adrian, Texas [AD, Head Basketball, Head Track, Head Volleyball] **Adrian Middle School-Adrian, Texas [AD, Head Basketball and Head Track]**

Midland High School/6A/ Midland, Texas [Head Golf Coach, assistant basketball coach]

Albany High School/2A/Albany, Texas [Head Boys Basketball, Head Golf, Head Tennis, assistant track] **Albany High School, Albany, Texas [AD, Head Football Coach] Van High School**

Van High School/ 3A/Van, Texas [Head Basketball Coach]

Hereford High School/4A/Hereford, Texas [Head Basketball coach and assistant football coach]

Permian High School/6A/Odessa, Texas [Head Basketball and assistant football coach]

Borger High School/5A/Borger, Texas [Assistant football coach]

Midland Junior College- Midland, Texas [Head Golf for both Men and Women and assistant basketball coach]

Odessa Junior College- Odessa, Texas [Head men's basketball coach] **Odessa College-Odessa, Texas [Head of Community activities- administrative position]**

Wayland Baptist University/D1 [NAIA]/Plainview, Texas – [AD, Head Men's basketball coach]

Kilgore Junior College- Kilgore, Texas [Head Men's basketball coach]

South Plains Junior College- Levelland, Texas [Head Men's basketball coach] **South Plains College- Levelland, Texas [Dean of Men-administration]**

Trinity Christian High School/Private school/Lubbock, Texas-[AD- Head Boys basketball]

Howard Junior College of San Angelo-San Angelo, Texas [Physical education instructor]

Stanton High School/2A/Stanton, Texas- [Head Girls basketball, assistant cross- country coach, Head Golf coach [BOYS AND GIRLS], assistant boys basketball coach and assistant football coach]

Robert Lee High School/1A/ Robert Lee, Texas-[Head Boys basketball, Head Golf coach [BOYS AND GIRLS], assistant middle school and high school football coach

Ozona High School/2A/ Ozona, Texas- [Head Boys basketball coach and assistant football coach]

Howard Junior College- Big Spring, Texas-[Head Women's basketball coach]

Wellman Union High School/1A/Wellman, Texas- [Head Girls basketball coach, Head Cross Country coach, assistant football coach, assistant track coach and Head tennis coach] **Wellman Union Middle School-[Head Girls middle school coach and Head tennis coach]**

Levelland Independent School District/4A/Levelland, Texas- [Bus driver for all sports teams]

St. Michaels High School/3A/ Santa Fe, New Mexico- [Head Boys basketball and assistant football coach]

Texas Tech University Athletic Department/NCAA D1/Lubbock, Texas - [Senior advisor of external facilities]

Trinity Christian High School/Private school/Lubbock, Texas- [Assistant boys' basketball coach]

Shallowater High School/2A/Shallowater, Texas- [Volunteer assistant boys' basketball coach]

Kirkland Central High School/4A/Kirkland, New Mexico- [Head Girls basketball coach] **Kirkland Central Schools-Kirkland, New Mexico- [Head of Alternative school administrative position]**

Trinity Christian Middle School-Lubbock, Texas [Head Middle School Boys Coach]

Trinity Christian High School-Lubbock, Texas [Head Junior Varsity Boys Coach] **Trinity Christian High School-Lubbock, Texas [Head Girls basketball coach]**

Jemez Valley High School/1A/ Jemez Pueblo, New Mexico [Head Girls basketball coach]

All Saints School/Private school/Lubbock, Texas- [AD, Head Middle school football and basketball]

Lubbock Christian University/NCAA D2/Lubbock, Texas [Volunteer Coach men's basketball]

PR Leyva Middle School/Middle school/Carlsbad, New Mexico [Head Middle school basketball coach]

Lubbock Christian University/NCAA D2/Lubbock, Texas [Volunteer men's basketball coach-statistician coach]

Trinity Christian High School-Lubbock, Texas [Volunteer girls' basketball coach-statistician coach]

CHAPTER ONE

COACHING LESSON-ONE

PUTTING LABELS ON STUDENTS IS A NO-WIN DEAL FOR THE STUDENT

ODESSA, TEXAS   AUSTIN ELEMENTARY SCHOOL

I will remember my first day of school in Odessa, Texas for the rest of my life. My parents enrolled me as a second grader at Odessa, Texas since I did not finish the school year at Kent, Texas **[population 75]**. Before school, I visited with Susan, my girlfriend and she told me that she hoped we would get into the same classroom. I remember she had this pretty pink dress with a pink bow tied around her ponytail. There was no doubt in my mind that she was the prettiest girl in the school, much less the second grade. I was so excited. Finally, the bell rang, and we all went to our respective rooms. The tardy bell rang, and the announcements began with the principal welcoming us to school that morning. After the announcements and the pledge, our teacher, Mrs. Reynolds, assigned me a desk to sit in. I had a brand-new desk that smelled of freshly cleaned wood; it was shiny, like the surface had just been varnished. I loved my new desk and I kept thinking about how lucky I was to be here. After we were settled in and Mrs. Reynolds had taken our roll, our class and the other two second grade classes assembled in a large room where chairs were placed into three distinct sections of the room. I noticed that all the seats were set in semi-circles separated from each other. Then someone started calling out names and placing students in different seats in different circles. My name was finally called out, and I had to take a seat in one of the outside semi-circles. **Once we were all settled, I remember to this day what happened next. The lead teacher began "Now students, this will be your seat for this semester in reading." She went on, "This group [pointing to the middle circle where Susan was sitting] will be called the blue birds; they are the fastest readers. The group in the outside circle on the left will be referred to as the "red birds"; they are the next-fastest readers. Two boys in my neighborhood were in that group. Then she pointed toward our group and said, "The group on the outside circle on the right will be referred to as the yellow birds. They are the slowest readers." Suddenly, it hit me like a rock to the head: I was dumb. It had never entered my mind until that very moment. I looked over at the two groups and it seemed as though my group had a dark cloud over us. It was raining with storms all around us. Their group had clear skies; the sun was out and there were no clouds. Susan was a blue bird, and my two friends were red birds. I felt embarrassed and did not want Susan to see me in the yellow bird group. I wanted to like Susan, but now that was not possible. I felt inferior for the first time in my life. The desk that I loved so much turned stale, the teacher, Mrs. Reynolds, was mean, and I was a yellow bird. My first day in a real school "taught" me that I was not good enough.** Putting labels on students in all walks of life is common in our day today. People are grouped into categories. It seems to make life easier for those in leadership roles so that they know how to respond when working with certain types of personalities and people. We do it by race, intelligence, physical abilities, physical appearance, money, power, and even where we live. A coach that puts negative labels on students for whatever reason has already failed that student before any teaching or coaching takes place. The damage that you do by putting any kind of negative label on a student does more harm than all the good coaching that was done before the label existed.

COACHING LESSON – TWO
GRACE
KENT, TEXAS

I was raised by my grandparents when I was in the first and second grade. There were thirteen brothers and sisters on my mother's side of the family. So, including me was not a problem. During that time, I had a naive attitude that all things are good and that we should all seek the best in each other. I loved my aunts and uncles like brothers and sisters. We would get so excited if one of the older uncles or aunts came to Kent, Texas [**population seventy-five**] to visit the family. We knew watermelon or home-made ice cream would be on the plate soon. We never talked about anyone in a bad way or even remotely questioned people of different colors. After all, we were in the minority being Anglo in Kent because most of Kent was made up of Hispanic culture. In fact, my best friend, who was Hispanic, was our neighbor. He had a sister that I thought was beautiful. The first time I used a phone, I was at the service station in Kent, Texas on the pay phone when I talked with my mom, who was in Odessa, Texas at the time. No one knew what a TV was at that time, nor did we care. Our playground was simple and fun. In the afternoons, after naps, often we would play card games or board games. **My problem was that I always tried to cheat to win, and my grandmother would get after me hard. She made it clear that my behavior was not acceptable, but she never made me feel like I was** a loser. What made me so lucky was that in this Boyd's house, there was love, compassion, caring, and truth, but never did I ever feel out of place or inferior to others.

COACHING LESSON-THREE
CREATE A FAMILY ATMOSPHERE
KENT, TEXAS

Ronnie was raised in a family environment of love, compassion, and acceptance: Ronnie received the best education a young child can receive in one way, but he also missed out because Kent couldn't provide the academic education Ronnie needed. A good coach needs to surround their team with a family atmosphere and those coaches that do that are always successful.

COACHING LESSON- FOUR
PEER LEARNING
KENT ELEMENTARY SCHOOL

I was lucky because I lived a wonderful childhood life in Kent, Texas. The school house was a one-room school with six grades. The first row was the first grade; the second row [where I was assigned] was the second grade; and so on for six rows of grades. My favorite aunts were the Boyd twin sisters Joy and Jolly and they were in the fifth grade. I was in heaven with all of us being in the same school. I thought my aunts were the greatest, and I tried to be just like them. Little did I know they were teaching me about love, acceptance, discipline, work ethic, pride, and most importantly, just having fun being me. I was the lucky one because I received positive peer learning in the best way possible.

COACHING LESSON-FIVE
FINDING OUT WHAT GIVES YOUR STUDENT A SWAGGER
ODESSA, TEXAS

Lucy's [my aunt that lived with us in Odessa, Texas] boyfriend was a strong, good-looking cowboy that rode an eighteen-wheeler into the neighborhood. That eighteen-wheeler receives lots of attention – good and bad but it did give Ronnie some swagger in his neighborhood. One of the keys to being a good coach is your ability to find what gives your players a swagger. When you do that, you have the advantage in coaching. You can't find out if you don't explore, ask questions, and listen. Information is critical to knowing the players you are coaching. If you search, you can find it, but you must search.

COACHING LESSON-SIX
YOU LEAD BY BEING AN EXAMPLE
ODESSA, TEXAS

Ronnie's uncle, Howard, [who also lived with us in Odessa, Texas] put Ronnie in a trash can upside down, hanging by his feet, because he was angry about Ronnie's work ethic. Yet, Ronnie wanted to be just like Howard, with no hard feelings about being put in a trash can. Ronnie admired Howard's work ethic. Howard worked hard at everything he did, which lead to success most of the time. Every wonder why some coaches can discipline players then those same players still follow and love that same coach? It's called leadership through example [walking the walk]. Talking the talk will get their attention, but walking the walk will get them to follow you.

COACHING LESSON-SEVEN
NEVER JUDGE A BOOK BY ITS COVER
ODESSA, TEXAS

Ronnie thought he was dumb because standard educational tests indicated that Ronnie was slow, much less being tagged as a yellow bird. On the other hand, in another environment, Ronnie was anything but dumb. His imagination was brilliant. He didn't know it at the time, but Ronnie did have an outstanding imagination. That imagination is still one of his assets in his life. Ronnie's dad was drafted in baseball by the Los Angeles Dodgers out of high school. Because of that he was a baseball nut, and developed a baseball game inside his house. He collected ballpoint pens and marbles and his collection was good. In his collection he had a great variety of pens and marbles. He would gather up eighteen pens and name them according to the batting averages listed on the sports page for the Brooklyn Dodgers and the New York Yankees. Each pen was different, and using his imagination. He would give a certain looking pen the name of a certain baseball player. He knew the batting averages of all the Dodgers and many of the Yankee players by memory. Then he would gather shoes from the closets and create a baseball park with a fence, backstop, and even out of bounds. The pitcher was his right wrist using his thumb and a finger. My left wrist, using a golf grip on one of the pens, became the hitter. Using only his right wrist and fingers, he could pitch a marble like a real pitcher does in baseball. Then he would hit the marble with my left wrist and finger combined, using a pen. After playing for hours, he started to get pretty good at pitching and batting. Then he would take my mother's house shoes and put one between first base and second base and the other between second base and third base. If he hit the marble into my mother's house shoes, it was an out. The only open area would be down the middle, which would be a "Texas League Single", or down the first base line, or the third base line. To make the outfield real, Ronnie added three cooking pans. He would place one in each outfield, and then if he hit the marble into one of the pans, it would be an out. If he hit the marble into the outfield and it didn't go into the pans, it was a hit or a double, depending on whether the marble went all the way to the fence line, which was made up of shoes. He could also strike-out but didn't do it very often. He didn't know it at the time, but he was having fun with statistics. He would make sure that the biggest pens were for the players that had the highest batting averages, and the smallest pens were the ones that were associated with the weakest batting average. He knew most of their batting averages, home run counts, runs batted in counts, and getting on base counts. He kept a notebook and kept up with my pen batting averages, home runs, doubles, and RBI's. He found this to be fun and he played this game for many hours at a time. He learned about strategy by playing the highest percentage player in order to win. He couldn't have had any better training for my coaching career, but in school he felt dumb. A coach must always strive to figure what rings the bell for athletes that are underachieves in the academic arena. When students underachieve, there is a reason, and it is the job of the coach to find out why. To do just that, a coach has to do something that is most difficult for all educators to do. They must open their minds to the situation. The question has always been and will continue to be, "Can a blue bird [the best rated students] relate to a yellow bird [lowest rated student]?" If you ask a blue bird if they can, they will say yes, but if you ask a yellow bird that question, they will say no. A good coach must carry an attitude to help his players that are underachieving in the academic area.

COACHING LESSON-EIGHT
PLAY TO WIN-HAVE A PLAN
SANTA MONICA, CALIFORNIA   RACE TRACK

My dad loved horse racing, and we would often go to the races at several different places. It was an education for me to watch my dad in action at the racetracks. First off, the night before the races, he would buy a racing form and would study it for hours trying to decide which horse was going to win each race. **He would tell me it was like playing baseball. You have to decide on the best percentage for winning** and go with it. He would look at so many different categories that I couldn't keep up with his thinking, but I sure learned what he was saying. **He would tell me that I had to learn how to play to win because that was what life was about. He would say always figure your best chance percentage wise and go for it. What always surprised me was that he seemed to have an ace in the hole. If his horse didn't win, he had** another horse set up in case it didn't pay. He almost won every time, and it made a huge impression on me. **He told me to always have a plan "B" and even a plan "C" if necessary, but don't be afraid to fail. Did he** give me great advice or not? The same is true of a coach. They must teach that playing to win and giving YOUR BEST **is winning regardless of the outcome.**

COACHING LESSON-EIGHT
SEARCH/SEEK DIFFERENT WAYS TO REACH OUT TO YOUR PLAYER'S YOU ARE COACHING
ODESSA, TEXAS

Ronnie takes swimming lessons from his coach at the public swimming pool. Ronnie is impressed with how his coach handles the differences in the abilities of all the young swimmers. Some are afraid of the water, some can float, some can swim a little bit, but all are different. **Developing strategies for different levels of players is difficult** and sometimes almost impossible. **It's a win-some lose-some category, and it requires a great deal of patience from the coach. It's one thing to** talk about it, but another to actually do it. That is what always upsets me with coaches, old or young. Every player you are coaching is different, with different needs and different values. As a coach, you must commit yourself to learning ways to meet the needs of each player you are coaching. If it was easy, then everyone would be a great coach. No, it is hard and sometimes impossible, but you must keep on trying in order to teach them how to achieve success. The lesson Ronnie learned from his swimming coach says it all. Find a way to relate to all your players. You say how? I say work at it, learn, and then apply what you learn. Get out of your comfort zone and try something new but learn from what you do and keep on trying. You keep learning every year, and eventually you will be able to really help all the players if you learn as well as they learn.

COACHING LESSON-NINE

NEVER FORGET THAT BOYS MATURE LATE/GIVE THEM A CHANGE TO MATURE

ORLANDO, FLORIDA

In the eighth grade, Ronnie and family moved to Orlando, Florida. They moved into a rented house by a lake. His dad received a job as a supervisor at a Tractor Supply Store. His boss had a son named Topper that was in the seventh grade, then Ronnie's was introduced to him. Topper lived on the same lake as Ronnie's, but Topper lived two miles away from where Ronnie lived. Ronnie's body started changing and he became stronger, faster, and more confident. Swimming all day long and swimming two miles a day started to make a difference in his muscular make-up. Coaches need to always remember that boys mature late most of the time, and what you see in middle school is not what you are going to see in high school. Don't allow the pressure to win determine your attitude towards young boys trying to make the team.

COACHING LESSON-TEN
WHAT IS THE PROPER WAY TO CUT A PLAYER FROM THE TEAM
SAM HOUSTON JUNIOR HIGH SCHOOL
AMARILLO, TEXAS

Ronnie gets cut from the team in the eighth grade. He is broken up because he didn't see this coming, and his spirit is totally wrecked. Coaches need to keep in mind one golden rule when they have to cut the team down to workable numbers. Treat the players you cut just like you would treat your own child. When you do that, you will make a losing situation better, although no one wins when a coach has to cut players from a team. Here are some guidelines: 1st [Make sure to announce the selection in a private setting if possible]. 2nd [Have a game plan for the future of the players that YOU are going to be cut in order that they might make the team next year]. 3rd [Take the time to do it right, meaning make an evaluation on paper with notes and check points about why you are cutting a certain player]. 4th [When you have to cut players, don't just do it by yourself but get some help so that you can get another opinion along with yours].

COACHING LESSON-ELEVEN
REAL COACHING IS UNSELFFISH IN ACTIONS NOT WORDS
SAM HOUSTON JUNIOR HIGH
AMARILLO, TEXAS

RONNIE's first coach to really make a difference in his life was Coach Teal. All Coach Teal did was direct Ronnie in an unselfish manner, which happened to be what was best for Ronnie instead of what was best for Coach Teal. Amarillo was a big football city, and football came first in every sport at Amarillo High School. That is why all the better athletes play football instead of basketball. Coach Teal knew that because he was the Head Football Coach at Sam Houston Junior High School, which was one of the main feeder schools in the Amarillo High School system. Ronnie wanted to play both football and basketball but both sports had a spring training, which meant he had to choose. Ronnie went to Coach Teal for advice. Coach Teal told Ronnie that his best chance to play sports at Amarillo High School would be basketball. He told Ronnie all the guys that were going to play football next year and Ronnie knew all of them. For sure, they were the best athletes in the school. Coach Teal told Ronnie that right now, he wasn't the athlete that the other guys were but when you graduate, my guess is that you will be one of the best athletes in Amarillo High School. For him to stick his neck out and recommend a young boy to play basketball was an unselfish act because he knew if Ronnie did turn out to be a really good athlete, Coach Teal would hear about it from the top and not in a positive way. Actions always speak louder than words.

COACHING LESSON-TWELVE

EVALUATION MUST BE OBJECTIVE AND NOT SUBJECTIVE/ THEN SHOULD PROVIDE A LESSON FOR THE PLAYER

AMARILLO HIGH SCHOOL

Ronnie's Junior Varsity coach developed a system of determining who was going to start each game by a "Performance Grade Sheet". It was a system where you received pluses and minuses for how you executed and finished plays during the game. If you made a field goal, it was worth two points, but if you missed a field goal, it was a negative one point. similar points for rebounds, steals, assists, and free throws. The final analysis was an objective-based performance evaluation. All coaches must evaluate performance because that is part of your job as an educator. The key to evaluation is consistency and fairness. Ask yourself, do you allow prejudiced feelings when you evaluate? Of course, you say you don't, but most coaches are prejudiced about something in their evaluation. Most of the time, they don't realize it and even defend their attitude if confronted. If you have ever been a SLOW LEARNER, you would know what I am saying is correct. Make your evaluation as objective as possible because subjective evaluations lead to misunderstandings that interfere with the achievement of the athlete. You need to put the player first and develop a way that you can evaluate a player in a fair way where your attitude doesn't reflect back on the players that fail. Coaches may be the most scrutinized people on earth because they get judged by everyone, not just the students and parents, but everyone in the community. It depends on the community, but usually the community creates pressure on the coach to win. With that said, coaches have a tendency to play to win and sometimes sacrifice life principles in order to win. Their evaluation depends on their ability to evaluate an athlete in stressful situations and then make a final determination about that student athlete. It is impossible for coaches to evaluate correctly when they are under stress except to rely on their own personal background and environment. That is why coaches must establish a method of evaluation that is objective and not subjective.

COACHING LESSON-THIRTEEN
ITS NOT WHAT YOU DO BUT RATHER HOW YOU DO IT
AMARILLO HIGH SCHOOL

Under Coach Hull, the team did the same drills every day. They were good drills, but something was wrong. To obtain success, it's never going to be what you do but rather how you do it. You are the deciding factor in the educational process. Communication is a must. It sounds simple, but it is not as simple as one would think. **You must learn to communicate what you are doing, why you are doing something, and finally, how to do it. Without that process, the student learns only what the student can imagine. Your ability to communicate is the key to what you are doing**, and everyone has a little different twist to their style of communication. In coaching, creating a drill that is competitive is instrumental to successful performance in the game. **Drills need to be competitive so that the players learn the process of competition, good and bad**. Games are the pinnacle for players, and the more a player sees competitive drills that create game-like attitudes, the better they will respond in games.

COACHING LESSON-FOURTEEN
DO YOU HAVE A CONTROL ISSUE
AMARILLO HIGH SCHOOL

Let the players play the game in games, Coach Hull never said a negative word, but instead just let the players play basketball. But he stood up for what was right and what was wrong. Coaching basketball players in games should be kept to an absolute minimum. In my opinion, coaches need to take charge and coach their teams like their lives depended on it in practice, but then become cheerleaders in games. I am not saying that you need to stop making critical decisions, but what I am saying is that you need to let the players play the game. As much as you want, you can't play the game for them, so you need to understand that they are doing the best they can. If it is not good enough, then you need to go back to practice and correct it. Ask yourself- do you really think that a player enters a game with the intent to make a mistake? No, you really don't think that way, but something happens to you in a game where you feel you must say something. What happens-your ego gets in the way, then you correct and criticize, trying to motivate them not to make a mistake. Most often, you make it worse.

COACHING LESSON-FIFTHTEEN
LEARN TO KNOW WHEN TO OPEN YOUR MOUTH AND WHEN TO KEEP IT SHUT
AMARILLO HIGH SCHOOL

The best coaches are the ones that can communicate-communication is a skill, and most coaches don't work at it like they should. Ronnie is coached by Gibb Ford, who is the student assistant coach at Amarillo

High School. Gibb was an outstanding all-American basketball player who played at Oklahoma State. Ronnie learned that learning from an experienced player that played at a high level was exciting and gave him a new level of confidence. He also learned the difference between learning from someone that could communicate verbally and someone that couldn't communicate very well. The difference was that he did not have to guess what was being taught but knew the minute Gibb Ford opened his mouth to speak. Work on your COMMUNICATION SKILLS. Learn to communicate with all kinds of students.

COACHING LESSON-SIXTEEN
BE CAREFUL ABOUT MAKING DEMANDS ON YOUR PLAYERS THAT ARE CREATING A CONFLICT WITH PARENTS
AMARILLO HIGH SCHOOL

Coaches are the world's worst at demanding something from a player when the demands are a conflict with the player's parents. Most of the time, parents will have the final say when this happens. I'm not saying that you should cater to the parents, but you should think before you make demands on an athlete, without knowing what you just demanded will conflict with the parents. The athlete might go along with the coach but in the long haul, the coach will lose. All coaches become better coaches, once their child begins to compete in athletics. Then, all of a sudden, they start understanding what parents feel when there is a conflict.

CHAPTER TWO

COACHING LESSON-ONE
FAVORITISM IS NEVER A SECRET   TCU [D1 NCAA]

Ronnie was entering his first registration in college [TCU] and the process scared him. He found out that the coaches helped Phil Reynolds, his roommate, and that hurt him deep inside. Coaches need to always be aware that when they demonstrate special attention to another athlete, the word travels faster than the internet between players. There is an old saying that covers this problem very well. It goes like this: "An ounce of loyalty is worth a pound of cleverness." Never do something special for one player that you would not do for the worst player on the team. Remember that concept and you will never go wrong.

COACHING LESSON-TWO
WHY TAKE IT OUT ON THE STUDENT-JUST BECAUSE YOU DON'T LIKE ATHLETICS   TCU [D1 NCAA]

Ronnie and Phil were told by the [TCU] coaches and some upperclassmen that some college professors resented students who were athletes. They were told to avoid those professors. As long as I have been in the athletic business of coaching, this has been a problem.

Teachers sometimes resent athletics—and not just for one reason, but for many reasons. As a coach, you will face this wherever you coach. The best way to handle it is to kill it with kindness. You're not going to change an attitude like this, but you don't want your players to suffer because of you. That is why it is best to just be kind and have compassion for such negative thinking.

COACHING LESSON-THREE
ACTIONS SPEAK LOUDER THAN WORDS   TCU [D1 NCAA]

Going from Coach Hull [high school coach] to Coach Brown [TCU coach] was a shock for Ronnie because Coach Brown was totally opposite in character and knowledge of basketball. Ronnie is adjusting to the difference between his high school coach and his college coach. The use of profanity in coaching is nothing but an admission of weakness. Regardless of how funny or powerful you think you are by using profanity, you are headed in the wrong direction. Some players can handle it and some can't. Why put the athlete on the defense by using words that tear instead of build? You are supposed to be in the business of positive education, and what kind of education are you providing when it is based on four-letter words that destroy confidence? Your actions speak so much louder than your words, and this story tells it all. If you want to drink and smoke, that is your business, but if you want to lead in a positive way, then you need to think seriously about your lifestyle. Always think about the example you are presenting when you are coaching, regardless of the situation.

COACHING LESSON-FOUR

EGOTISTICAL COACHES FORGET WHAT COACHING IS ABOUT   TCU [D1 NCAA]

Ronnie was surprised at how negatively other players on the team reacted to Coach Brown's [TCU Coach] methods of coaching. For him, Coach Brown was like a **basketball god because** Ronnie had never really had a true basketball coach. This may be the greatest coaching lesson that exists in the world. Coaches need an ego and need confidence in order to do a good job of coaching. It is necessary because of the environment that surrounds all coaches trying to do their job. Listen to what I am saying and this will help you the rest of your career. What coaches don't need is for you to be so egotistical that you miss out on what is really important to the end result of your coaching. I really see this in experienced coaches, especially those that have won some championships. Styles of play and systems of play can be different for many different kinds of coaches. When a team wins a championship, the coach usually gets the credit. Because of that, sometimes coaches get egotistical in the process of winning. This means just what it says; the coach becomes full of himself, completely self-absorbed. How else can you describe Coach Brown's behavior? It goes with winning, and coaches that follow that pattern miss out and soon develop an arrogant attitude. An arrogant attitude is defined as an adjective to describe people who are too proud and look down on others. Phil and Jerry had a hard time making the adjustment between their high school coach and Coach Brown. They simply couldn't do it, because of Coach Brown' egotistical attitude and his arrogant way of handling those two athletes. Coach Brown missed out, and they missed out, but who do you blame? Who is the leader? He was right in one way but totally wrong in another, and because of that, true communication between the two ended. This was a war between coach and player that didn't really have to happen. But it does happen each and every day of the year in many schools where the biggest problem with coaching is the ego of the coach. That is why it is so hard for some coaches to understand this concept. Coaches have a bad habit of believing that they are the reason the team wins. In reality, talent is what decides who wins. Coach Brown had a style, a system, and a way of communicating. Coach Brown won when he had talent and he lost when he didn't have talent. Communication between player and coach is critical to the success of both, but often the coach forgets this concept because of ego. Just like coaches want basketball officials to leave their ego at the scorer's table before the game starts, coaches need to put their ego in check or in the closet when the game starts, **all good coaches have a strong ego, but the good ones know when to get rid of it, and the poor ones carry it to their grave.**

COACHING LESSON-FIVE

THERE IS ALWAYS ANOTHER LEVEL OF PLAY-YOU JUST DON'T KNOW IT   TCU [D1 NCAA]

TCU won the Southwest Conference and then was defeated by Cincinnati by a score of 84-65. Ronald thought that TCU would defeat Cincinnati without a problem with Kenneth Kell guarding the All-American Oscar Robertson. That night, Ronnie learned that there are different levels in basketball, and TCU was not on the same level as Cincinnati. He was amazed at Oscar Robertson and how athletic he was, along with his skills in basketball. You see, this was the first time Ronald had witnessed a black athlete playing basketball vs. TCU. He saw with his own eyes the difference between Kenneth Kell of Avoca, Texas, and the All-American Oscar Robertson. It made him aware of different levels of play in college basketball, which, up to that point, he thought were all equal. He found out that night that all was not equal. What he wanted to know is how you get your program to the level of Cincinnati.

COACHING LESSON-SIX
FORGET THE PAST-LOOK TO THE FUTURE-COACH THE PRESENT TCU [D1 NCAA]

Ronnie makes a 2.9 after the first semester at TCU: This is the greatest example of what is wrong with our school system. Why did it take all these years before Ronnie felt he had success in a classroom environment? The majority of his teachers didn't work hard enough to really understand his inferior attitude toward his academic background. The coaches at TCU made him feel good about what he was doing in the classroom. The coaches at TCU accepted him for what he accomplished in his first semester at TCU. They never looked at his past, nor did they care that he was a slow learner. What they cared about was his performance in the classroom now, and he was at the top of the freshman class in grade point average. Ronnie even started to think he was smart. It was the first time in his life in an academic environment that he started to think that he was normal. Coaches don't evaluate from the past, but from the present.

COACHING LESSON-SEVEN
A COACH INSPIRES THEIR PLAYERS TO BE BETTER
TASCOSA COUNTRY CLUB, AMARILLO, TEXAS

Ronald was fascinated with the Head Golf Pro teaching golf lessons. He studied his technique and why he was so successful. A good coach inspires their players to be better. You do that by talking the talk and walking the walk. First, the golf pro could demonstrate and correct in a gentle, non-threatening manner. He could talk the student through the process with a confident tone of voice. As he talked through the process, he made you feel you could do what he was asking. He had a system of coaching where he could relate to different types of skills when teaching. But what he put emphasis on when coaching was the fundamentals of the golf swing. Then he would explain and demonstrate what he was talking about. He would start with the grip, then the stance, then the alignment, and finally the takeaway of the swing. He would explain that those are the basic fundamentals of the swing and when you performed those fundamentals correct, your chances of success are good in the swing pattern. Coaches often take short cuts in teaching fundamentals because they want to win. So, they spend most of the workout time working on how to win instead of teaching and working on the fundamentals of the game. It doesn't take a rocket scientist to figure out which players suffer the most when this situation happens in the coaching world. Non-athletes can't make it without fundamentals, and the good athlete will eventually play out when they face the same athlete with good fundamentals. If you don't feel comfortable with this issue, then ask some experienced coaches and let them mentor you, helping you do what is needed fundamentally for your players to get better.

COACHING LESSON-EIGHT

A COACH MUST DEVELOP A PLAN CONCERNING HOW TO HANDLE INJURIES   TCU [D1 NCAA]

Ronald hurt his ankle and it kept him from performing like he needed to perform in practice and games. He attempted to come back sooner than needed because he felt he was getting behind. The results were terrible and his confidence suffered when he went back on the court without healing the ankle properly. Every year you coach, injuries will be an issue unless you are lucky. Any kind of injury can affect the mind of the athlete, and the coach needs to understand that concept.

If a player is hurt, and it really doesn't matter what kind of athlete gets hurt, it is impossible for that athlete to return to normal play until the injury has had time to heal and the athlete has had time to regain the confidence that they lost during the injury. At this point in my lifetime as a coach, I have never seen an athlete that is exempt from injury. With that said, you, as a coach, need to develop a philosophy about how to handle injuries. If the athlete is normal, they will want to get back into competition quickly, but that is the worst thing you can allow to happen. A good rule of thumb is to always pay attention to a doctor or a trainer that specializes in injuries and the healing of injuries. Be careful about listening to the player that is injured.

COCHING LESSON-NINE
WHEN ATTEMPTING TO COACH A DIFFERENT CULTURE- NEVER FORGET TO STAY HUMBLE
AMARILLO CARVER SWIMMING POOL

Ronald had to teach the Carver Swimming Pool lifeguards how to teach swimming lessons. He was the only white person that had ever entered the Carver swimming pool. He was hired by the city of Amarillo to instruct the hired life guards at all the Amarillo City Pools how to teach swimming lessons, which included Carver Swimming Pool. The lesson to be learned in this story is so important and can really be an issue when coaching athletes of different cultural backgrounds. In our day and time, teaching students of different cultures is a daily experience. Today's world is different, but the reason that Ronald had success is not different at all. The life guards played a trick on Ronald and he had to jump into the water and rescue a young black child from drowning. Ronald was embarrassed, not really knowing if he had been set up or not. Then when the same issue happened again instead of jumping in to save the same black child from drowning, he told the group, "I guess we will have to let him drown". That broke the ice and from that point on, all was well and his instruction was absorbed by the black life guards. So, what can we learn from this story. To begin with, humility is the key when coaching players that have a different culture than you. It is normal for players of a different culture to have trust issues with a different coach. You can't afford any kind of arrogant attitude if you really want to relate to athletes of different cultures. Ronald jumped in the water, jumped back out after saving the kid and carried on as if nothing happened. He was embarrassed and he felt he was set up but he didn't jump out of the water swearing or yelling blaming anyone. Instead, he just kept his poise and started over. Ronald joined in on the joke the second time even though it was on him. Being humble is the key.

COACHING LESSON-TEN

WHEN PLAYERS FEEL THEY HAVE NO CHANCE YOU AS A COACH HAVE FAILED THAT PLAYER   TCU [D1 NCAA]

Coach Brown had a system where he would play only eight players, and if you wanted to play, you needed to get into that top eight, or you wouldn't get the opportunity to play once the season started. Coaches, this might be the worst characteristic that a player could say about you. You will not change. Ask yourself if you fit that bill. The truth is that I have seen many coaches that will not change regardless of the situation. It's a simple equation, so ask yourself if you would like to play for a coach that will not change regardless of what happens. This goes back to the thought that the system is more important than the player. When players feel they have no chance, you, as a coach, lose everything you are working for. Never forget that concept when you coach.

COACHING LESSON-ELEVEN
COACHES NEED TO BE AWARE OF NEGATIVE VERBAL COMMENTS THAT TEAR DOWN INSTEAD OF BUILD-UP
TCU [D1 NCAA]

Ronald hurt his left ankle in his senior year in exactly the same way he hurt the ankle in his sophomore year. He couldn't bounce back from the injury, and it destroyed his confidence, much less any chance of success. Coach Brown got angry and classified him as the greatest three-o'clock shooter in the world. For some of you to understand, that is saying that Ronald was a great shooter at practice but not during the games. Coach Brown didn't just say these things in front of the players, but in front of everyone at practices. Many times, that included the press and other important people that represented TCU. Of course, his nickname was still "The Little Shit." Coaches need to ask themselves what is being accomplished by tagging Ronald with a nickname that creates negative feelings and then delivering a verbal statement that tears down Ronald's confidence at the same time. If you ask yourself, "Is this coaching?" or better yet, ask yourself, "Do I do that to my players?" If you do, then it is time to stop coaching or change. Many coaches think they have to get under the skin of a player in order to get them to play at a certain level. In other words, make them mad or get them emotional about something so they can perform at a higher level of play. Bottom line, when a coach turns to that kind of motivation, both the player and the coach lose. It might work for a moment or a day, but the change will be only short-lived. Negative verbal statements that inspire always hurt more than help in the overall scheme of athletics.

COACHING LESSON-TWELVE
DO YOU HAVE A PASSION FOR BEING A COACH
TCU [D1 NCAA]

Coaching his fraternity in all sports made Ronnie feel good about himself, and not once did he worry about being a yellow bird. From this experience, he developed a passion for coaching that would carry him over the rest of his career. It helps in the coaching world if you have a strong passion for your job. If you don't have a strong passion, you might consider doing something else.

COACHING LESSON-THIRTEEN
FIRST RULE OF COACHING – LEARN TO LISTEN
FT. WORTH, TEXAS

That spring semester, AFTER BASKETBALL SEASON, I was asked to play basketball for a semi-pro basketball team in the Fort Worth area named "Frogs". The team was made up of older guys that played college basketball, mostly ex-TCU guys that lived in the Fort Worth-Dallas area, and two that played for the Dallas Cowboys organization. We played on weekends and practiced one night during the week, making it easy for all to participate. The main guy and money guy would provide free meals at his place called "The Burger Place". Most of the players on the team knew my complete story, and it made me feel special again. It was like an old reunion for me with all the ex-TCU guys and even the two pro football guys because they were ex-TCU football players. I went from not playing for TCU to averaging eighteen points a game for "Frogs". The only problem was my ankle would swell up like a balloon each game we played. I would put ice on it and the swelling would go down. Soon after I joined the team, our coach had to move to Atlanta because he was being transferred through his job. Since everyone on the team had a real job, they asked me to coach the team. I was the only one that had the time. Since my ankle was a problem, I accepted the position. The next day, I wanted to change my mind because it became clear to me that I was the youngest guy on the team and I had no experience other than coaching the fraternity guys at Phi Delta Theta. To be honest, I was scared to death. My first thought was how I was going to decide who starts and who subs. **That Sunday, I went to El Chico's to eat, which was located just around the block from the TCU campus. At a table in the middle of El Chico's was Bob Lilly, and he was by himself. Bob Lilly was an All-American football player at TCU and was in his first year with the Cowboy organization. I knew him well enough that I invited myself to join him. We started talking about our basketball season at TCU, and then we went into his first year as a Cowboy. He told me it was tough going at first and that he had to be alert and smarter about playing than he did at TCU. I was listening to him when [it hit me like a bell in my head] because he was telling me how Tom Landry, the coach for the Cowboys, made his decisions about who started and who played at his position. He told me that Landry used a grading system by grading the tape of the games in regards to how you performed on each play you played. If you did what you were supposed to do, you got a good grade, and a poor grade if you didn't do it right. Then he figured your percentage vs. good or bad performance and ended up giving each player a percentage grade. It was then that I remembered my Junior Varsity coach at Amarillo High School using his grading system to determine starting players and subs. As soon as I got back to the dorm, I called Coach Bacon. He was very glad to hear from me, and then, when I told him why**

I was calling, he got excited. He explained his grading system to me in detail, and I decided right then that I was going to use that system with my new coaching position. I went to work right away, thinking the system through by myself. I was going to use his system just the way it was because I remember it working for me. When I met with the team at practice, I explained my plans for deciding who starts. As I told them, I honestly couldn't say who the best players on the team were, so I felt we needed a system that could provide me with an honest evaluation where everyone had a chance to start. The team seemed to like the concept, but I could tell they didn't totally buy into it.

We had a young man that was part of the team but didn't play, and I declared him the statistician for our team. Some of the guys really didn't like him, and I must admit he was different. He always came with one of the players, and it appeared they were best of friends. We had our first game and we started with the guys that had been starting with the old coach. My plan was to get started with the grade sheet in my first game of coaching. After the game, I took the stats to my dorm and figured the grade for everyone. On **Wednesday night, at practice, I put the grade out for everyone to see. I am a naive person and I guess I will always be naive, but I was shocked that the majority of the guys were upset with the grades. The main issue was that they felt the statistician missed too much. They could remember more assists, more steals, more deflections, more rebounds, and more shots made and missed. But the main reason that they were upset is that our stat guy** didn't miss a **thing that happened to his friend, and some of the guys on the team thought that wasn't fair. For sure, I had a mess and it was up to me to figure it out because it was my concept to begin with. I told the guys on the team that I would figure it** out even if it meant that I had to do the stats. I started thinking about how we could keep our heads up and write down all that was happening on the court. Then I remembered my younger days listening to the radio with my dad following the Dodgers game by game. My dad and I would keep up with hits, strikes, and balls and all the game stats by listening to the radio. That is when it hit me that if we used a tape recorder, we could keep our heads up and see the game at the same time. I was taking a speech class and we were using the tape recorder to listen to our own voices, trying to improve our speech. I went to see my professor, and she was very helpful when I told her what I wanted to do. She loaned me a really nice tape recorder. At our next game, I tried the tape recorder out and made my stat guy sit next to me. During the game, he would call out the game play by play and I would help him along the way. If I saw something that he missed, I would tell him, and he would record what I said. When the game was over, I went back to the dorm, listened to the tape, and graded the plays that the players made. **The difference between the two games was like night and day. The games with the recorder provided a more realistic evaluation, and they also provided me with instant feedback of what the players were really doing on the court. It was a more objective viewpoint, and it helped me make better decisions. At practice, the guys on the team were happier with the results, but they still thought the grade sheet needed to be more about winning than just getting a grade. In other words, they wanted more specific information on the grade sheet. Frustrated, I said, "If that is the case, then you decide what you want." We sat down as a team and we worked through the process. Here is what they decided:**

[Field Goals Made +2], [Field Goals Missed -1]- [If your shooting % was 50% or better, the Field Goals would be worth +3 instead of a +2] [If your shooting % was below 30%, then the misses would be a -2 instead of a -1] The thinking was that when a team shoots 50% are better their chances of winning are high.

The thinking was that when a team shoots 70% or better, their chances of winning are high. [Free Throws Made +2], [Free Throws Missed-1]; [If your free throw shooting was 70% or better, the free throw made would be worth a +3 instead of a +2]; [If your free throw shooting was below 50%, then the misses would be a -2 instead of a -1].

[Rebounds, whether on the offensive glass or the defensive glass, would be worth +2]. [Assists were worth +2 and turnovers would be a -2]. However, the most important issue was whether you had more assists than turnovers or more turnovers than assists. [It was decided that assists would be worth +3 if you had more assists than turnovers, and turnovers would be worth -3 if you had more turnovers than assists].

Then the discussion went to hustle plays. When asked what a hustle play was, it was defined as a play where the players' hustle keeps us from having a turnover or keeps the opponents from scoring. So, the terms "offensive saves" and "defensive saves" were developed. [A +2 would be given for a save].

[Then we went down the list and gave all the rest a +2]. That included steals, deflections, blocked shots and drawing a charge.

The next game we used the tape recorder in the same manner as before, but this time when I graded the tape it was clear who really helped the team and who didn't. I didn't say one word to anyone about the grade sheet, but I noticed an attitude difference in everyone about the grade sheet. I was surprised and to be honest, it

really helped me decide who to play and who to start and so forth. What even surprised me more was how the team started playing better basketball. We started to become aware of what was good and what was bad in a game. Even to the point of making fun of the grade sheet. A player might get a steal and when he passed by the bench, he would say +2. It really helped our attitude as a team, and we really developed into a good team and won most of our games. One thing is for sure, it was about as good of an education as I could get as a coach.

CHAPTER THREE

COACHING LESSON-ONE

YOU NEED TO WORK AT TEACHING JUST LIKE YOU DO COACHING

HEREFORD HIGH SCHOOL   4A

The first thing a young coach has to learn is that they are going to be judged by their teaching more than their coaching. That is hard to accept since you will be spending twice the time coaching as teaching, but it is what it is and the sooner you understand that, the better off you will be. Teaching is critical to your success as a coach. Here is a story I would like to relate to you: Early in my career I was teaching in a high school of about 1100 students. I had two biology classes and two health classes and was also the head Boys Basketball coach and assistant football coach. That spring, I was told I would have a student teacher helping me in my health classes. The first day my student teacher was supposed to report to me, he was late. The problem with being late was that we were having a film that would last about 20 minutes, and since he was late, I didn't have time to explain what we were doing or what I expected from him. He arrived just as we were about to start the film. I always give my class a pop test concerning the film when it is over. Then we use that film for discussion. During the film, I heard someone snoring, so I turned the lights on. To my shock and surprise, it was my student teacher. The next day, my student teacher was given the keys to the classroom, a book to study, and a roll book, and was told the class now belonged to him. He looked surprised, but he was smarter than the average young coach. He knew I was not a happy camper with him sleeping in my class, much less coming in late. He wasn't about to say anything. I told him if he needed anything, I would be in my office. I left and said "good luck." If you don't see anything wrong with his attitude towards the classroom, then you are the one that I am talking to. His clear attitude of disrespect in the classroom is what gives educators the perception that coaches think they are above the rules just because they are coaches. He wouldn't be late for practice and he wouldn't sleep at practice. But that student teacher was a little different and ended up being one of the most successful athletic directors in the state of Texas. I hope I taught him a valuable lesson. Teaching is part of your job, and you need to excel at it if you want to keep your job.

COACHING LESSON-TWO

LEADERS ARE IN CONTROL, PREPARED READY FOR THE BATTLE
PERRYTON JUNIOR HIGH SCHOOL   3A

Both Mr. Mayberry and the principal were sitting down in the principal's office with the troubled student when the principal reaches behind his desk pulling out a huge paddle. The student refuses to be paddled. Mr. Mayberry is new to this type of situation so he doesn't know what to expect or how he should act. The principal goes to the phone, calls the probation officer and then turns to the student telling him, he can go back to the detention center in Amarillo or take the paddling. Think about this next statement. Mr. Mayberry is EIGHTY-FOUR years old and he still remembers that principal. What he remembers most is the way the principal handled the situation. He was in control. The key to this story is that the principal knew what kind of student he was dealing with. Because of his knowledge, he knew how to handle the situation. His education about this student helped him keep his school from being intimidated by this student. Leadership at the top is critical in the educational process. When Mr. Mayberry went back into his classroom, the atmosphere was totally different, it was more positive for Mr. Mayberry which gives him a better opportunity to really do his job. That atmosphere was created by the principal. As a coach you are going to be challenged in many different ways and in order for you to handle those challenges you must have a philosophy and a guideline for yourself in handling problems just like the principal. How he did that was through experience and knowledge about his students. His experience told him what to do and his knowledge told him how to do it. It is the same in the athletic arena.

COACHING LESSON-THREE

COACHES ARE ABOUT BEING A POSITIVE EXAMPLE/THAT IS HOW THEY LEAD

PERRYTON JUNIOR HIGH SCHOOL   3A

Mr. Mayberry was lucky to be surrounded by two excellent coaches in his first year. Although Mr. Mayberry didn't coach in his first year, he learned from two of the best by watching and observing both coaches during the school year. The junior high basketball coach was Jim Reid, and the high school basketball coach was Roy Pennyton. They both won state basketball championships in Texas, but what impressed Mr. Mayberry was how they conducted themselves. Both coaches were first-class people, humble individuals, and great teachers. He couldn't have had a better example to follow. Coaches that rebel from being under the micro-scope of the public shouldn't even think about coaching. A coach is expected to be a leader and set a good example for students to follow. If that heat bothers you, then get out of the kitchen.

COACHING LESSON-FOUR
PROFESSIONALISM IS THE BACKBONE IN THE EDUCATIONAL SYSTEM

Mr. Mayberry received great recommendations from his high school coach, his college coach, and his first superintendent. Mr. Mayberry was too inexperienced in the education business and was naive about obtaining a job, but one thing he didn't do was undermine his superiors. Regardless of the circumstances, he was raised as a child to respect-authority. Coaches and teachers must learn to be loyal, but most importantly, they must learn to keep their mouth closed when they don't have something positive to say about their bosses. Again, it's called professionalism and it will either break you or make you.

COACHING LESSON-FIVE
MENTORING NEEDS TO BE HONEST AND TO THE POINT PERRYTON
JUNIOR HIGH SCHOOL   3A

Mr. Mayberry went to Coach Jim Reid for advice and encouragement concerning applying for a coaching and teaching position. Coach Reid was brutally honest, and his comment took the wind out of Mr.

Mayberry's enthusiasm for the job. Coach Reid was not putting anyone down, but rather he was giving Mr. Mayberry the cold, hard facts that he needed to hear. As a leader in the coaching business, we sugar coat too much for our young coaches. We need to be realistic and honest so that coaches can understand what they are dealing with instead of having a wonderful day dream turn negative. Give your young peers hope, but be clear about the challenges they will face.

COACHING LESSON-SIX
THE KEYS IN AN INTERVIEW FOR A COCHING POSITION
ADRIAN HIGH SCHOOL   1A

Mr. Mayberry was asked by the school - board what he would do if he was selected as the head basketball coach at Adrian High School since he had no experience. Mr. Mayberry was honest and answered the question with a question. He wanted to know what they wanted in a coach. After they answered his question, he told them he wasn't sure what he would do, but he was really sure that he knew what not to do. When you interview for a position, it is most important that you come across as sincere and humble. You need an ego and you need to be confident, but it needs to be put in place at the right time or you will blow your opportunity during an interview. If you blow your horn too much, you might get the job, but now you have to live up to all the smoke you were blowing. It is best to be honest and humble. Then, if you get the job, you can be yourself, and your chances of success are much greater.

COACHING LESSON-SEVEN

A COACH IS HIRED TO DO THE JOB, NOT QUESTION THE JOB ADRIAN HIGH SCHOOL   1A

Coach Mayberry was required to drive a school bus in the mornings, starting at 5:30 a.m. He would pick up students, arriving just in time for school to start. It was a seventy-mile round trip. Then he had four different classes, all requiring different preparations: two athletic classes, one in junior high and one in high school. He would drive the same bus route that he drove in the morning, which meant that he drove 140 miles that day. He was also the athletic director for the school, which led to duties he handled when he returned from the afternoon bus trip. He had extra duties as a coach at the high school and junior high school levels that kept him busy at least four nights a week. He was making $4,500 and he thought he had died and gone to heaven. One of the biggest problems a coach will face in a school system is jealousy. Many educators think that someone else has it better than they do, when in truth, no one individual has it better than the other. Everyone is expected to do their job and not be looking over their shoulder, guessing who might have a better situation, meaning class load, student ratio, salary, scheduling, subject matter, and extra duty. A coach is hired to do the job, not question the job. When a coach does the job, they are hired to do, they don't have time to second guess what is going on with another teacher or coach. If you have the attitude above, you need to quit or change your behavior because your attitude will reflect back on your coaching, which will affect the athletes you are coaching.

COACHING LESSON-EIGHT
THERE IS NO SUBSTITUE FOR ENTHUSIASM IN A COACH
ADRIAN HIGH SCHOOL   1A

Ron Mayberry was a popular hit at the Adrian school system even though it was his first year, even though he had no experience, and even though he was learning as he went along. The key was his enthusiasm and energy. Those are the two keys for success in coaching at any level. What one needs to remember is that when you gain knowledge and experience, don't let that take the place of enthusiasm. There is no substitute for enthusiasm. It is critical to the learning process of any student or athlete.

COACHING LESSON-NINE
WHEN CHALLENGE-STAY HUMBLE AND PICK YOUR TIME TO ANSWER THE CHALLENGE
ADRIAN HIGH SCHOOL   1A

Coach Mayberry was challenged in both his biology class and on the basketball court by one specific individual. One of the biggest lessons in teaching and coaching could be in this paragraph. One of the better basketball players and also one of Coach Mayberry's favorite students/athletes challenged him in Biology class about the characteristics of fish. The biology book stated that all fish had scales as one of the outstanding characteristics. One day in class, Mack Simmons questioned the book, saying that catfish don't have scales because he had caught a bunch of catfish of which none had scales. Coach Mayberry really didn't know how to answer that because he was not a fisherman, so all he could really do was just turn the cheek and go another direction. Then, in basketball,

Mack challenged Coach Mayberry about running lines, pretending that he didn't understand. This is the lesson, so listen. In class or in athletics, you are always going to be challenged by someone. You never really know the intent of the challenge, so you must always remember not to get defensive but rather listen to the challenge and respect the challenge. This will give you time to determine what direction you need to go. Always buy time for yourself before you respond. Most importantly, waiting until your opportunity to respond is where you are going to make an impression on the challenger. You need to pick the time and not let the challenger get under your skin. Mack was a good person and a good athlete, but he had a rebellious side to him. Instead of getting upset with Mack about the question of scales on catfish, Coach Mayberry told Mack that he didn't know that because he had never been fishing. The class couldn't believe that Coach Mayberry had never been fishing. Then Coach Mayberry reminded the class that he was a city boy and didn't understand much about farm life or fishing. Well, he got the subject off the catfish deal, but when Mack challenged Coach Mayberry about a running exercise called "lines" in basketball class, everything changed for Coach Mayberry. Mack had just given Coach Mayberry the opportunity to get Mack's attention. That is what happened, and that situation happens all the time in a classroom or in the athletic arena. The point is to don't lose your cool, bite the bullet, and then wait for the opportunity to get your point over. You will have a higher chance of winning the war, maybe not the battle, but the war.

COACHING LESSON-TEN

THE REAL DEAL IS A HOME VISIT-IT IS A WIN-WIN DEAL FOR A COACH

ADRIAN HIGH SCHOOL   1A

Coach Mayberry was trying to understand his players better in order to help them become better basketball players. The problem was he lacked experience on how to do that. He read in a Texas Coaching magazine about a coach that made home visits with the players on his team. The purpose was to get to know the players better and to gain the support of the parents. Coach Mayberry experimented with having home visits and the positive results of the home visits changed his coaching philosophy. If I had a suggestion for all the administrators, I would tell them to require coaches to do just what I did. In an article from George Mason University recently, a professor of education stated: "Many people see smaller class sizes and more money as part of the general solution to our nation's educational problems. It turns out that since 1955, the average number of students per teacher has fallen from twenty-seven to sixteen. During the same period, real per-pupil expenditures have increased more than fourfold." There is only one thing that can help a coach relate to athletes and that happens to be hard work concerning everything about the athlete. When you visit a student in their home with their parents, a different environment is created. First, the gloves are removed, then the parent and child feel comfortable in this environment. Second, you are not going in to tell the parents about something their child has done wrong, but instead you are trying to understand their child in order to be a more effective coach for their child. Third, when you direct your attention to the well-being of their child, the attitude of the meeting totally goes in a different direction, especially toward you as a coach. In my experience, any expense or effort a coach has will be worth home ***visits.***

COACHING LESSON-ELEVEN
UNDERSTANDING THE COMMUNITY WHERE YOUR PLAYERS LIVE WILL HELP YOU RELATE TO THE STUDENT YOU COACH
ADRIAN HIGH SCHOOL   1A

I called a Saturday workout my first year at Adrian. It was October 15, the day we could start working out after school. One of my best players, Robert Perry missed the workout. He was a great kid and to be honest, it shocked me that he would miss a workout. When I asked him why, he said that he has to work at the farm on Saturdays. I asked Robert is he minded if I talk to his dad about missing our workout. Robert got excited about that and set up a time for me to visit his dad. But the problem was that the next Saturday was the only time, his dad could visit with me so I called off practice and went to Billy's house Saturday. Of course, what I didn't realize is that almost everyone in Adrian knew about what was going on with this situation. I had no clue but learned about it later on after I left Adrian. When I arrived, I knocked on the door, and his mother answered the door. She was very nice and then told me that they were expecting me but Billy and his dad were already out in the fields working. It was 7:45 a.m. and I thought I would catch them at home. She told me where they would be and told me to go join them. When I found them, they were working on a barb wire fence, and it was clear that they were focused on their work. I walked all the way up a hill, and Robert saw me and waved. His dad didn't notice me at all, but he was busy. When I got to their pickup, Robert's father yelled at me and said, "Glad you could make it. Will you bring that large wrench by the driver's seat to me." I did as he said and when I handed the wrench, he asked me if would go over to where Robert was located because he needed some help. That morning, I learned how to set up a barb wire fence. I found out that it is a hard job and one that demands you pay attention. The clock turned to 11:45 a.m., and Robert's father yelled, "It's time to eat." I looked at Billy and he told me that his mom was cooking some good food and he would ride with me back to the house. I figured that I would get around to talking to his father after lunch. The lunch was out of sight; chicken fried steak, mashed potatoes, green beans, corn on the cob, ice tea, cream gravy, and homemade apple pie. It was the best meal I have ever eaten in my life, and as soon as the meal was over, I wanted to take a nap. After the meal, Mr. Perry went to the bathroom, and I started talking to Mrs. Perry. I was so full, it was hard to even think, but I was determined to talk to Mr. Perry. Next thing I noticed was that Billy was missing and then Mr. Perry didn't come back into the dining room. Mrs. Perry told me that they went to take a nap and that I should do the same. I had come this far, and I was determined to talk to Mr. Perry, so I just sat down on the couch. Soon I was asleep. When I woke up, both Robert and Mr. Perry were already out in the field so I had to go find them again. When I found them, they were working on a water tank that they used to water the animals on the farm. I watched them from a distance for a long time before I got out of the car and walked toward them. When I was close enough, I could hear Mr. Perry talking to me. He said that he didn't want to wake me up because I was snoring loudly. I asked him if there was anything I could do to help. He told me to come over to his side so we could talk. He was very nice, telling me he appreciated my coming to the house, eating with the family and helping with the fence. I told him that it was an education for a city boy like me. He laughed out loud and he said to me, "So you want Robert to come to practice on Saturday's during this basketball season?" Then he added "Do you know that the last coach that asked the players to do that got fired!" I said, "I didn't realize that and this experience was new to me." Then he said, "I hope you understand what Robert does on Saturday and how important his work is to our farm and our life style." Then he said, "Billy will be at the next Saturday practice." I couldn't believe what I was hearing, but I had some time to really think about this situation, particularly when I was watching them work while I was in the car. I told Mr. Perry, "You don't have to worry about him being at practice, because we are no longer going to have practice on Saturday." I continued, "It is clear to me that those boys are needed at home more than in the gym." Then I said, "Thanks for teaching me a hug, lesson." We shook hands and I went back into Adrian smarter than I was before.

COACHING LESSON-TWELVE

YOU CAN LEARN FROM EVERYONE IF YOU OPEN YOUR MIND AND LISTEN

ADRIAN HIGH SCHOOL   1A

Coach Mayberry learned by watching the girls' basketball team play six on six. Really, it was three on three, and he was impressed with how much easier it was to score on the offensive end when you don't have five on five. This thought helped him to understand both offense and defense. Coach Mayberry had never watched girls play basketball, but from watching the girls play, he learned that the three defensive girls on one end had a hard time guarding three offensive players. The bottom line was that there was not enough off-side help defense. Of course, when you added the other two defensive players, then the offense became harder to execute. From this observation, Coach Mayberry learned the basis for good offense [proper spacing] and good defense [proper spacing]. On offense, the object is to create space in order to take away defensive help, but the object on defense is to take away space in order that players can help more quickly. The point here is that coaches never need to quit learning and they can learn from someone that they least expected to learn from. The biggest threat to a coach is a lack of time or desire to learn something new.

COACHING LESSON-THIRTEEN
ONE OF THE GREATEST FRATERNITIES IS THE COACHING FAMILY

Coach Mayberry learned this when he starting calling other coaches for help. He needed to know the best way to attack a match-up two-three zone and a one-two-one full court trapping defense. What he found was that he had a pipe line of people that wanted to help and offer opinions about different ways to attack both defenses. Coach Mayberry was lucky in the fact that pride never got in the way of his desire to win. You see, he was a yellow bird, so he was used to that kind of thinking. But what he found was a gold mine because he joined a huge fraternity called coaching. If you are a blue bird and you have too much pride to ask for help or, more importantly, to know you need help, then you are headed in the wrong direction. Coaching just might not be for you. And guess what coaches, when you don't attempt to learn because your pride gets in the way of learning, you will be OK, but your players are hurt and that is the reason you have a job.

COACHING LESSON-FOURTEEN
THE ULTIMATE REWARD FOR COACH
ADRIAN HIGH SCHOOL   1A

Coach Mayberry told the Adrian Superintendent that he was going to accept the coaching/teaching position at Midland High School, then he went to play golf in Amarillo, Texas, forty-five miles away from Adrian.

Just as he is about to tee off on the first hole, Coach Mayberry notices several guys walking toward him. When Coach Mayberry realizes that those guys coming toward him were his Adrian basketball players, he knew why they were at the golf course. Coach Mayberry breaks down, crying, knowing they are here because the Superintendent told them he was leaving. Every person involved with the achievement of athletics can identify with this scene. It doesn't happen often, but when it does, it makes everything that you do in the athletic arena worth it. From a coaching standpoint, all the wins in history can't duplicate the positive emotional feedback he received by seeing those guys coming all the way from Adrian. He broke down and cried, then hugged each one, telling them how much he loved them. Now that is what coaching is all about.

CHAPTER FOUR

COACHING LESSON-ONE
THE GREATEST LESSON A COACH CAN LEARN
MIDLAND HGH SCHOOL   6A

Coach Mayberry was mentored by Jay Spears, who was the Head Boys Basketball coach at Midland High School. He taught Coach Mayberry the greatest lesson that a coach can learn. It's not what you do but rather how you do it, and it's not about what you know but rather what you can coach. Every coach in the world attempts to copy successful coaches in basketball. You ask yourself why? It's simple. When a coach has success in winning games, it is only natural to think it is because of what they are doing. So, they attempt to duplicate exactly what someone else is doing. I have a good friend named Mike Mitchell who was an excellent coach. He won a national championship at Western Texas College, a junior college in Snyder, Texas. He was a masterful coach of the one-three-one zone. He was in high demand to give clinics on that defense. I used to attend his clinics and enjoy his demonstrations. After the clinic was over, coaches would go back to their regular coaching positions and attempt to coach that same defense the way he described the defense in the clinic. Somehow, that defense never worked out the same way that coaches perceived it would when they were in the clinic. That was because it wasn't what he was doing but how he did it. Mike's articulation was superior to most coaches I know. He was super intelligent, and his vocabulary was excellent. He had a way with words and voice commands that could get anyone's attention, much less a group of basketball players. If he told them to go from point A to point B and if they didn't do it the way he thought they should, players would be exposed to his articulation. Trust me, none of his players liked to be on his bad side. So, you can see what I am getting at, because of his ability to communicate, not the defense. The defensive players were good. If a coach didn't know Mike, they would never pick up on that concept, but if a coach watched his workout, any coach would understand why his players reacted the way they did. Mike was a masterful communicator, and that was his strength. **Now, the problem with this concept is that sometimes it leads to lazy coaching. The excuse is that "I don't know how to coach it," so I just don't try. There is not a coach in the world that doesn't use that excuse, and it borders on lazy thinking. The question is not whether you can coach it, but rather whether it will help your players get better or gain an edge in the competition you are playing. If you can gain an edge for your team and your pride gets in the way of progress, then you are the one that is holding your team back.**

COACHING LESSON-TWO

COMPETITION DONE RIGHT CAN BE A STRONG MOTIVATION FOR IMPROVEMENT

MIDLAND HIGH SCHOOL   6A

Coach Mayberry used competition to motivate his golfers to work on the little things that were so important. Coach Mayberry quickly realized that he was not qualified to help his golfers with their swing or even mental approach to the game of golf. Each player had a golf professional to help them along the way. So, what he tried to do was help the golfers with the little things in golf, such as mental toughness and practice habits. He would develop individual games on the greens and at the practice range that helped with practice so that the golfers didn't think it was work but fun. He developed a ladder for putting, driving, approach shots, sand saves, chipping and match play. A ladder is one of the best ways to individualize competition. An example would be if you have eight golfers and you need to find a way to establish which players are ranked one through eight. The best way to do that is to have a contest and rank them according to how they finish in that contest. Then on certain days, the even numbers challenge the odd numbers. Winners move up and losers move down. Then change it up and have the odds challenge the evens. This helped coach Mayberry keep it interesting. Then he made them practice during cold weather, which he felt helped their mental toughness. The lesson is that you, as a coach, can coach any sport if you will apply yourself to the little things, particularly the little things that you understand.

COACHING LESSON-THREE
EVERY COACH NEEDS A MENTOR
MIDLAND HIGH SCHOOL   6A

Coach Mayberry is deciding on whether to accept a coaching position in Albany, Texas. He asked his mentor for advice. Coach Mayberry's was an excellent mentor because he told Jay Spears the truth about coaching in Texas. Coach Mayberry was naïve about the entire process of advancement in the coaching world in Texas, and Coach

Spears told him what he must do in order to advance. He told him he needed to learn how to coach football if he was to advance, and Coach Spears was one-hundred percent correct. Coach Mayberry didn't know it at the time, but that advice turned out to be the major advantage Coach Mayberry had over other basketball coaches for the rest of his high school coaching career. The next year, Coach Spears went to New York and became a stock broker. For the most part, it is still the same way in Texas. If you want to advance, learn how to coach football.

COACHING LESSON-FOUR

COACHES NEED TO LEARN HOW TO TAKE CARE OF THEIR FACILITIES

ALBANY HIGH SCHOOL CLASS   2A

Coach Mayberry received a master's degree in coaching football, but it wasn't what he thought it would be. Coach Mayberry learned how to mark a football field, how to move sprinkler pipes in order to keep the football field in good shape, and how to air up blocking dummies by putting covers on them. That was his first exposure to football. The lesson here is simple. We all need to learn how to take care of what we use and be more responsible for what happens to our facilities. Football coaches learn that because they are expected to keep their facilities up-to-date. How many times have you cleaned and even washed a basketball court? If you have, then you have learned a great lesson. If you are a basketball coach, the first person you need to take care of is the janitor in charge of the gym. Treat them well, respect their job, and you will be thankful in the long run. Don't allow your players to disrespect that position.

COACHING LESSON-FIVE
ALL COACHES CAN LEARN FROM EACH OTHER
ALBANY HIGH SCHOOL   2A

Coach Mayberry was impressed because each position coach would take turns explaining the coaching techniques in football, and how to develop those techniques in practice. The best thing about this type of introduction to football was that I could learn from each coach that was making a presentation. Each coach had a certain style, and each coach had their own unique personality. Each coach was given chalk and asked to demonstrate on the chalk board what they were talking about. It wasn't just the football information that was digested by Coach Mayberry, but also the style of coaching coming from each different coach. The lesson for basketball coaches is to think twice before refusing to coach football. Football coaches are intense coaches, and you can learn from each one. Basketball coaches are the world's worst at isolating themselves away from everyone. Join the group and learn from others as well as yourself. Learn to take the good and forget the bad. It doesn't matter how much you know but rather how much you can teach. One of the biggest lessons to learn in coaching or teaching is that you need to coach what you can and stay away from what you can't.

COACHING LESSON-SIX
IT DOESN'T MATTEER HOW MUCH YOU KNOW, BUT WHAT DOES MATTER IS HOW MUCH YOU CAN COACH
ALBANY HIGH SCHOOL   2A

The example in this paragraph was how Coach Mayberry coached the little things in football such as: Off sides, getting the snap count right, knowing when to be on the field, taking too much time in the huddle, getting to the line of scrimmage in a lazy manner, getting plays mixed up, and avoiding penalties. This was what Coach Mayberry meant by "coaching the little things." People get caught up in saying, "I don't know much about that." When in reality, they know more than they think, and what really matters is what you can teach, not how much you know.

COACHING LESSON-SEVEN
RESPECT MUST BE DEMANDED IN THE ATHLETIC ARENA
ALBANY HIGH SCHOOL   2A

Coach Mayberry was addressed as "Ronnie" by two senior football players in practice. When he corrected them, they continued to address him as Ronnie. The lesson learned in this paragraph is the word respect, and that word is so important in the coaching business. Players that don't respect you are going to be difficult to coach. I had an AD - coach tell me in an interview that it was more important for the students to like you than respect you. I liked what he said, but I knew that he had never been in an environment coaching nothing but yellow birds. Later, I learned that he had never been in the classroom period. Respect comes from being prepared for the situation that presents itself. Just remember, you will always have a few that are going to challenge you, most of the time in an accidental manner, but you must respond in a positive way. I am not saying you enter an athletic arena with a chip on your shoulder but you should be alert and responsible in the environment you are working.

COACHING LESSON-EIGHT
EAT YOUR PRIDE-FIND THE RIGHT TME – THEN CONFRONT
ALBANY HIGH SCHOOL   2A

Coach Mayberry is taking inventory of his basketball equipment in order to know what to order for the coming year. Football is one week away from being over then when two student athletes grab a basketball and start shooting in the gym. Dee, the Head Football coach gets mad at Coach Mayberry. He tells him to stop those guys from shooting and put the basketball up. Coach Mayberry does what he is told, but he is very upset with Dee about the way he acted. Coach Mayberry never told anyone this story, and he waited until the proper time to approach Dee about this situation. The lesson to learn is this: Regardless of how wrong you think your superior happens to be, wait for the proper time to discuss or confront your boss. Confrontation in the heat of the battle will get you fired every time.

COACHING LESSON-NINE
COACHES NEED TO LEARN TO ADAPT TO THEIR PLAYERS
ALBANY HIGH SCHOOL   2A

Coach Mayberry realized that his team was not very good but none of the teams he had to play were very good. Do you remember the lesson Coach Mayberry learned from his dad about playing to win. That was exactly what Coach Mayberry did when he taught his players a one-three-one zone but in practice and worked on man-to-man defensive principles. Instead of being prideful about playing man to man defense, he played a zone because it gave his team a better chance to win. Coach Mayberry wanted to play man to man defense but he knew his players had no background in that kind of defense, so he worked daily on the man-to-man defensive concepts but in games, he played a zone in order to give his team the best chance to win. He had three days before his first game. In other words, Coach Mayberry adapted his desires in basketball to what the players could do, but never did he give in to his desire for them to play man-to-man defense. Coaches need to learn to adapt to players more than the players need to adapt to the coach. This philosophy is not accepted by most coaches, and I think it is a mistake.

COACHING LESSON-TEN
THE KEY TO WINNING IS GOOD LEADERSHIP
ALBANY HIGH SCHOOL   2A

Coach Mayberry coached a golf team to a state championship, but he learned a huge lesson in the process. Coaches have a hard time understanding why their team struggles when they shouldn't. Also, coaches wonder why their team is inconsistent and plays up and down so much that the coach gets frustrated, the players get frustrated, and the community gets frustrated. The answer is leadership, and after fifty-three years in the coaching business, I can honestly say that I have never had a good team without it. In this example, Herbert Hawkins was the leader on the golf team. Also, he was the best player, and that should go hand in hand, but often it doesn't. He influenced the players on the team not to take their driver to the State Tournament in order that they could keep their score within what was needed to win. He gave up his own desire to be the long hitter by the driver, and feel that sensation of power off the tee. He also knew that the driver created more problems than it was worth in order to have a score that they could win. He influenced his fellow players to do the same by making them think it was their ideal. That is leadership, and all teams that win have it in some shape or form. Coaches always try to determine who the leaders are, but often they fail because true leadership is silent when it is time to be silent and vocal at the right moment. Poor leadership is easy to see and we, as coaches, try to eliminate poor leadership, but the truth is it is hard to eliminate. Most of the time, poor leadership happens when coaches aren't around and when they least expect it. So, the bottom line is the fact that if you know you have poor leadership and you don't do anything about it, then you are part of the problem.

COACHING LESSON-ELEVEN

COACHES MUST STEP UP TO THE PLATE AND DO YOUR JOB- DON'T TAKE THE EASY OUT

ALBANY HIGH SCHOOL   2A

Coach Mayberry knew the time had come to approach Dee Windsor, who was the Athletic Director, about the basketball program. He knew what needed to be done in order to improve the basketball program. Coach Mayberry knew that the players needed the opportunity to get better and he felt responsible. He also knew that Dee could easily find another basketball coach. With that in mind, Coach Mayberry used diplomacy and careful wording in order to communicate with Dee. So, what is the lesson in this paragraph? Most people go with the flow. They remain in misery, sadly accepting their security while avoiding the risks required to make their dreams a reality. When you see a coaching opportunity for the growth of students, you must step up to the plate and be a leader. Most important to remember is that leadership requires a full commitment from you. When Dee gave Coach Mayberry a reason for not accepting his program, Coach Mayberry answered with a total commitment, accepting the fact that he would have to make the commitment above the call of duty.

COACHING LESSON-TWELVE
THE GREATEST TEACHER YOU HAVE IN COACHING IS YOUR OPPONENT
ALBANY HIGH SCHOOL   2A

I have learned everything from the coaches I have coached against. They have been my #1 teacher, and you are a fool if you don't learn from your opponents. I could write a book just on that subject alone. Coach Mayberry was the lucky one again. He was coaching his defensive tackles in a football scrimmage with Stamford High School. Stamford was led by a legendary coach by the name of Larry Wartes. Coach Wartes and Gordon Wood won State Championships at Stamford like we drink soda pop. He immediately felt a different kind of attitude within the coaching staff and the players on the Stamford team. Stamford had an assistant coach named Larry Dippel, and Coach Mayberry really liked the way he addressed the players during the scrimmage, but he couldn't define what he felt. What is the lesson in this paragraph? Learn from others and be open to different ways of coaching. Coach Mayberry had never been exposed to what he was feeling coming from the coaches at Stamford High School. He felt the chemistry between the coaches and the players on the Stamford team, and it was a new experience. Learning from your opponents is the lesson if you can't figure it out. Yes, even if you don't like them. Learning to humble yourself is a coach's nightmare. Another example was when I was coaching in a tournament and I felt we had better players, but we got outplayed and outcoached. The team was Hawley, located just outside Abilene with very few students attending the school. In fact, they were in the lowest class in Texas, called class "B". Albany won the game, but Coach Mayberry knew they were lucky and felt bad about the fact that he really didn't know how to counter the defense he witnessed. It was a triangle and two. What that means is that Hawley's defense played two guys man -to- man and played a zone on the other three guys. Soon, Coach Mayberry started working on that type of defense in order to learn how to attack that particular type of defense. Coach Hull, his high school coach, used to do the same thing. He would make them execute something so that they would learn how to play against it. What he found out was that this defense could be used as another weapon to win games. The lesson in this paragraph is to always learn from your opponent. "Pride is a cruel enemy. It inflates our personal importance and makes holiness impossible." Pride can be a coach's nightmare, but if you will humble yourself and admit that you made a mistake and throw pride out the window, your growth as a coach will also grow. Don't let pride get in the way of making your players better. That is a sin in the coaching world.

COACHING LESSON-THIRTEEN
DON'T WAIT-AN ADMINISTRATION CERTIFICATE IS A MUST ALBANY HIGH SCHOOL   2A

Coach Mayberry is encouraged by the top two administrators at Albany to go back to school and get his administrative certificate. Coaches need to be required to go back to school and begin their administrative degree. Not only does that give coaches a well-rounded education, but it prepares them for the future when coaching is not an option.

COACHNG LESSON-FOURTEEN
PROFESSIONAL COURTESY IS PART OF PROFESSIONALISM

Coach Mayberry has been recommended for a head basketball position at Van High School, Van, Texas. The recommendation comes from Coach Brown who had been the basketball coach at Van for over twenty-five years. It was a tradition that Coach Brown decided which ex-TCU player would be the next coach. Coach Mayberry and his wife declined the offer without visiting or talking to the school administration. Instead, he listened to his old friend, who happened to be the ex-coach at Van High School. When someone recommends you for a position in the coaching or educational arena, you owe it to the person that recommended you to show respect by at least visiting with the school authorities about the position. It's called professional courtesy.

COACHING LESSON-FIFTHTEEN
YOU DON'T HAVE TO LIKE ALL YOUR PLAYERS BUT YOU NEED TO LOVE ALL OF THEM
ALBANY HIGH SCHOOL   2A

I was named the Athletic Director and Head Football Coach at Albany. At the same time, I was offered the Head Basketball position at Van High School. Van was a step in the right direction, where I might be offered a position as a college basketball coach. We accepted the offer at Van, and now we had to tell the Albany Administration. I loved coaching at Albany, loved the students, parents, athletes, the city, and the school board. Leaving Albany was hard. I had already called Buddy Dulin, one of my best friends at Albany, who was now the Superintendent. Of course, that made it harder, but at the same time easier. I was close to Buddy, so I could really open up about everything, but I hated to put Buddy in this position of having to hire a coach at such a late date. He seemed to understand, and we set up a time for me to turn in my resignation on paper. He asked me when we were leaving Canyon [I was working on my administrative certificate at West Texas State] so that he would be at the office when we arrived in Albany. We were about ten miles from Albany when I noticed a long line of cars coming toward us with their lights on. I didn't know what to make of it until they got close enough and then I recognized who was in the cars. It was my entire football and basketball players from Albany packed in cars coming to meet me. I pulled over and got out of the car. Each car, about eight to ten cars, turned around and came back up the highway beside me and pulled over on the other side of the highway. I honestly didn't know what was happening as they got out of their cars and came toward me. No one said a word, but they stopped in front of me and threw the football notebook on the ground, then left without a word as they got back into their cars and left. I was stunned and cried like a baby. I loved those guys and it hurt me deeply. In front of me on the ground were about thirty notebooks, so I picked them up and my wife and I went into Albany to resign my positions as Athletic Director and Head Football Coach. Later, that night the entire group came by the motel I was staying in to say good-bye. The lesson in this is to speak from your heart and the players will respond. You don't have to like all of them, but you need to love each one. To this day, I still have contact with several of the guys on that team.

CHAPTER FIVE

COACHING LESSON-ONE
BE WHO YOU ARE AND NOT SOMEONE ELSE WHEN YOU COACH VAN HIGH SCHOOL   3A

Coach Mayberry struggles with coaching at Van for the first time in his lifetime. He is mixed between trying to continue the coaching philosophy that has been successful at Van and his own coaching philosophy. He is not happy with himself and feels he is doing a terrible job of coaching. Every coach that coaches, has a difficult time with the same issues that Coach Mayberry was fighting. For sure, if they are coaching at a school that has strong traditions of winning. Coaches, the rules are simple. For one, a coach must be himself or herself and not attempt to be like someone else. That doesn't mean that you don't copy and learn from someone else, but a coach must find a way to coach that fits their personality. Two, a coach must continue to learn and absorb concepts and methods. Quit making excuses for not learning. Young coaches use enthusiasm, have lots of energy, and often provide a strong motivational influence over the players that they coach. Old coaches have a strong habit of relying on old methods to win games, particularly x's and o's. What a coach must work for is a balance of learning but not getting out of their positive personality traits. Three, the best coaches are the ones that learn constantly and adapt to different methods of the game but still coach within their personality. All coaches use the excuse that they don't feel comfortable coaching a certain type or method. Sad but true, applying what you learn is where real learning takes place, and it is also where coaches either go downhill or uphill.

COACHING LESSON-TWO

YOU WANT SUCCESS, STAY ON TRACK WITH WHAT YOU KNOW, THEN TRY SOMETHING NEW

VAN HIGH SCHOOL   3A

Coach Mayberry got back on track with home visits and getting to know the players and parents at Van. Although the culture was totally different, the home visits did the trick again because Coach Mayberry started understanding the players at Van better, which in turn created an opportunity to communicate what he was about. You can't work too hard at trying to communicate. One thing he learned is that the talent at Van was coming.

COACHING LESSON-THREE

COACH TO YOUR STRENGTHS-STAY AWAY FROM YOUR WEAKNESSES

VAN HIGH SCHOOL   3A

Coach Mayberry wanted to be a coach that understood x's and o's, but he just wasn't that type of coach at this point in his career. All young coaches want to understand and think they can be clever in coaching the x's and o's. I wasn't different, but when I got back into coaching through motivation, I did a better job. We must all coach to our strengths whatever that might be. That doesn't mean that you don't attempt to learn and grow as a coach, but you must always remember your strengths. Just remember that, usually, your strengths are also going to be your weaknesses. That is the hard part, and the sooner you learn that, the better coach you will become. A typical example would be similar to this statement. Our coach has an outstanding work ethic. No one outworks our coach, but sometimes his work ethic gets in the way of his being able to see simple things going on because he is so focused. It is like the coach can't see the trees for the forest.

COACHING LESSON-FOUR

EVERYONE IS ALWAYS LOOKING FOR A COACH THAT CAN DO THE JOB
HEREFORD HIGH SCHOOL   4A

It had been almost three years since Coach Mayberry had thought of Coach Wartes. Coach Wartes was the head football coach at Stamford when Coach Mayberry met him during a football scrimmage. Because of circumstances beyond Coach Mayberry's control, he was leaving Van and looking for a coaching job in the Amarillo area. Coach Mayberry contacted Dee Walker, who was the Athletic Director of the Amarillo Public School system. Dee told Coach Mayberry that he would get the word out, and soon, Coach Mayberry received a phone call from Coach Wartes. Coach Wartes had moved to Hereford, Texas, and was the Athletic Director at Hereford Public Schools. Coach Wartes phoned Coach Mayberry and all but offered him a coaching position at Hereford. Coaches, this might be the biggest lesson that exists for coaches. The coaching business is the only business that I know that you don't have to broadcast what you can do. Your peers already know what you can do if you are coaching. There are very few jobs that carry information about success or failure, like being a coach. Every night you play, you are being judged and your peers are paying attention. To be honest, your peers will usually be more accurate about the job you are doing than the people that hired you. You, as a coach, may think that no one in your area cares or is really interested. You might be right, but you can count on it that someone is watching and listening. You will never hear it, but good coaches know because it is in their best interest to know. That is part of the business we are in.

COACHING LESSON-FIVE

TALKING THE TALK THEN WALKING THE WALK CREATES AWESOME TEAM ATMOSPHERE
HEREFORD HIGH SCHOOL   4A

Coach Mayberry is driving a U-Haul moving truck from Van, Texas to Hereford, Texas. When he gets into the city of Hereford, Coach Wartes and his assistant coaches are on hand to help Coach Mayberry move his furniture into a rented house in Hereford, Texas. The bottom line to success in school business is teamwork, and the bottom line to believing you are on a team is walking the walk more than talking the talk. Actions speak louder than words, and Coach Mayberry felt he was part of that team by the actions of those coaches that were there when he needed them.

COACHING LESSON-SIX
WHAT MAKES FOR A GREAT LEADERSHP AT THE TOP HEREFORD HIGH SCHOOL   4A

Mr. Mayberry was introduced to his all-time favorite principal and assistant principal. He explains why those two are his all-time favorite leaders. In my opinion, the major reason I liked these two administrators is easy to define. They complimented each other in the way they led the school district, which gave the school district balance and fairness. Jerry Don George always had an open door and an ear for your heart. Mr. Mannerly would listen to you if you had a problem with a student, but other than that, he really didn't have time to listen to your heart. Mr. George was tough and always came across as fair, sometimes easy. Mr. Mannerly was tougher and didn't really care if he came across unfair. Business was business and his business was protecting the teachers and the students that wanted to learn. Mr. George was forgiving when a teacher made a mistake. Mr. Mannerly never held a mistake against a teacher, but he wouldn't forget. Mr. George would stand up for your program and take a stand for you, and Mr. Mannerly would do the same, except keep Mr. George in line so that he wouldn't go overboard defending you. But the factor that really separated those two is that they supported each other with words and actions. That is what made those two leaders so special. The same is true of the assistant coach. They need to support each other in different ways in order to help each other do a better job of their responsibilities.

COACHING LESSON-SEVEN
WHAT A CHAMPIONSHIP PROGRAM LOOKS LIKE FROM THE INSIDE
BROWNWOOD HIGH SCHOOL   4A

Coach Mayberry traveled to Brownwood, Texas to witness the Brownwood High School athletic program under the direction of Gordon Wood. Gordon Wood was a huge, legendary coach in Texas, winning more football games than any other Texas high school coach, and Coach Mayberry wanted to see firsthand what made his program special. Successful coaches are usually mentored by someone who was mentored by someone, and so forth. There are no secrets in the coaching business, but only about 10% of coaches are successful in terms of winning championships. Think about what I am saying here, coaches. Gordon Wood mentored Larry Wartes, and Larry Wartes mentored Larry Dippel. Larry Dippel won at Hereford and later at Amarillo High School, where he became a legend. Someone somewhere mentored Gordon Wood, and they all bought into a philosophy that helped them develop football players in order to win championships. Coach Mayberry learned a method of coaching that he didn't know existed when he visited Brownwood High School that spring day. It was an education in itself and something that he would use for the rest of his coaching life. What a championship program really looks like inside the program is priceless.

COACHING LESSON-EIGHT
NEVER FORGET WHY YOU WERE HIRED
HEREFORD HIGH SCHOOL   4A

Coach Mayberry finally understood that at Hereford High School, boys' basketball was just not important enough for the boys to make any kind of commitment in order to get better. He knew that it was going to create waves if he started to expect a commitment and he knew it was going to be a battle. Then he remembered why he was hired. Sometimes coaches forget that issue because they don't want to create negative waves, but you must always remember why you were hired and then go give it your best. The best rule of thumb is to remember that you must light your own fire.

COACHING LESSON-NINE
SOME PLAYERS NEED A STRONG PUSH IN ORDER TO BE EFFECTIVE
HEREFORD HIGH SCHOOL   4A

Coach Mayberry had a player named John McNey who he felt was an outstanding basketball prospect at Hereford High School. He was talented but had never been pushed hard enough to actually know how talented he really was. Talent is God-given and the gene for talent is not always dominant. In other words, the gene for a certain talent might be there, but you can't see it because it is not a dominant gene. That was the case with John McNey. Most athletes never reach their maximum ability level because they just won't push themselves that hard. It is human nature to take the easy way out if given the opportunity. Believe it or not, that is what you are supposed to do. John was normal, not abnormal, and it was my job to attempt to make John a better basketball player. I was going to have to push him, and if I expected him to like it, I would be crazy. I did push him and sometimes he would look at me like I was a crazy man, but he took all the push I had and he became the player he wanted to be. The proof was in the pudding because he received a basketball scholarship his senior year. He could honestly say he did the best he could do. The job of the coach is to get the player where they want to be as a player. It is your job to provide the environment and the extra push in order to get the player what he wants to begin with. If a player doesn't want the extra push, you will know quickly and you can back off that particular player. That doesn't mean you can't push someone else.

COACHING LESSON-TEN
SHARING ATHLETES IN HIGH SCHOOL-ONE BIG ISSUE
HEREFORD HIGH SCHOOL   4A

I was lucky because I had the best mentor-he could teach everyone something about sharing athletes. Coach Mayberry and Coach Wartes understood that if each program was going to be successful, they had to share athletes. Coach Mayberry really didn't know how to open up about the situation, but Coach Warts took the leadership role and helped him in the process: OK-Coaches, Athletic Directors, and Administrators, this is the big one. This is the issue that athletic directors, principals, and other administrators hide behind their desks and pretend this problem doesn't exist, but let me tell you right now, this is the biggest problem in high school athletics that does exist. It's called "Sharing Athletes" and it's like a cancer in an athletic program that just destroys all the good that coaches and players do. I was the lucky one at Hereford and now after thirty different schools that I coached in I know that for sure. So, what is the lesson that needs to be learned? Coaches are going to be coaches regardless of any situation, and it's up to the administrator in charge of athletics to control issues of sharing athletes. I wish it wasn't true, but coaches seem to have tunnel vision when it comes to sharing players, and that includes athletic directors that happen to be coaches. Matter of fact, often they are the worst because they have the power. In my case, Larry Wartes the Athletic Director and Head Football coach was the leader as he helped decide how we could share players. He took the lead and handled a situation that could have been bad, but instead he turned it around by making decisions that helped share players so the player was not put in the middle of a conflict between two coaches with different programs. That is what leaders do, and that kind of leadership is what makes a good athletic program.

COACHING LESSON-ELEVEN
ALL COACHES HAVE A JOB DESCRIPTION THAT ARE NOT WRITTEN
HEREFORD HIGH SCHOOL   4A

Coach Mayberry and the team make a commitment to basketball. One player, a returning starter, demonstrates no commitment even after Coach Mayberry explained what he wanted in terms of commitment. When your school hired you, the job likely came with a written job description, clarifying expectations. But the other job description, the one nobody outlines in writing, is the job you must do in order to accomplish the first job. In order to accomplish one of Coach Mayberry's written job descriptions, he had to take a stand against athletes that wanted to play basketball but weren't willing to commit to basketball on the terms that Coach Mayberry stated. It was a tough stand because he had a lot to lose, particularly his job. But he knew he was right and it was not personal but just a change that was needed in order for him to accomplish his job. Then he had a senior returning starter who he had to confront about his lack of commitment and told him that he wouldn't stop him from being on the team but he was not going to play him. He quit the team and then went to see his dad, who was the President of the school board, and because of that, created some problems for Coach Mayberry. Coach Mayberry survived, and the basketball program got better. Leadership starts with you, and sometimes you have to put your neck on the line to get it done.

COACHING LESSON-TWELVE

IF YOU DECIDE TO COACH, YOUR SPOUSE WILL BE CRITICAL FOR YOU TO HAVE SUCCESS-SHE NEEDS TO BE A TROOPER

Coach Mayberry has moved from Albany to Van and now he is coaching at Hereford. His brother, who is ending his ninth- grade year, lives in Gulfport, Mississippi, where the high school he was supposed to attend burned down in the summer. That means that he would have to attend another high school twenty miles from where he lived. It was clear that this situation was going to create a huge problem for Coach Mayberry's family and particularly his brother. Jeany, his wife, is pregnant, just starting a new job, has a two-year old to take care of, a new home, a mother that is very ill, and then tells Coach Mayberry that we better bring his brother into the family at Hereford. If you plan on making a career out of coaching, you need to make sure that your spouse is ready for everything you are going to have to handle. Bottom line: your spouse will determine your success, so when you make that decision, you need to keep that in mind. Coach Mayberry was the lucky one.

COACHING LESSON-THIRTEEN
HOW DO YOU COACH YOUR OWN BLOOD
HEREFORD HIGH SCHOOL   4A

Coach Mayberry has a brother that will be a sophomore in high school and he is transferring from Gulfport, Mississippi to Hereford, Texas. His brother's name is Mike, and he wants to participate in basketball in Hereford. Mike isn't coming to be the star basketball player but just to be part of the program. Mayberry explains to Mike in terms that Mike can understand how he must be treated in order to get the respect of his teammates and coaches. Coach Mayberry tells Mike he has three options and he needs to choose which option he wants about how Coach Mayberry should treat him as a basketball player. The lesson he had to learn is that he is not like any other basketball player because he is Coach Mayberry's brother. Because of that fact, everyone will treat him differently, even though he will be the same. They will see him from a different viewpoint. Some will think he is given special rights above other players regardless of how Coach Mayberry and Mike handle the situation. That is human nature and is a natural response from parents and players. Coach Mayberry is just giving Mike a heads-up on what is going to happen and letting him decide between three options how he wants to be handled. Mike chooses the last option, which is the toughest of all, but will demand that everyone respect Mike and learn to love him for who he is instead of what they think he is. This is one of the hardest lessons in coaching, and that is how to coach your own blood. What makes it hard is the fact that no one particular way is right because of the individuals involved. Coach Mayberry knew Mike was going to have a hard time because of his size. He was small at 5'7", but he was a very good basketball player with a high IQ for basketball. The problem was the competition for his position was tough. He didn't need any help from Coach Mayberry in order to gain respect and confidence from his teammates.

COACHING LESSON-FOURTEEN
DO NOT BABY YOUR BEST PLAYER-DON'T FAKE IT-MAKE IT REAL-THAT IS IF YOU REALLY WANT THAT PLAYER TO BE YOUR BEST PLAYER HEREFORD HIGH SCHOOL 4A

Coach Mayberry coached one of the outstanding players in the panhandle of Texas while in Hereford, and he learned the most valuable coaching lesson that exists. If you really want your best player to perform, then you need to be harder on them than anyone on the team. Your best player will only be as good as you push that player, and babying that player is the worst thing you can do. You must always remember that the opponents are not going to baby your best player. If your best player rebels on you, then the one that you think is your best player isn't your best player.

COACHING LESSON-FIFTHTEEN
NEVER LOSE PERSPECTIVE ABOUT WINNING
HEREFORD HIGH SCHOOL   4A

Hereford basketball went from poor to really good in four years' time. Coach Mayberry, along with Coach Wartes, totally reconstructed the basketball program into one of the strongest in the Texas Panhandle/Plains area. Then, Keith Kitchens broke his foot just before district play started for the Whitefaces, who had a thirteen-one record. Keith was being recruited by several Division one coaches + Keith was recognized as one of the better players in the State of Texas. How good was Keith?

He didn't play in his district his senior year, but he was selected by the Texas High School Coaches Association to play in the Texas High School All Star game. At that time, that was the highest honor a player could get in terms of recognition. Coach Mayberry was about to learn the biggest lesson that life presented in the coaching world. It is the lesson that all coaches must learn and the most important lesson that exists in the coaching world. Coaching is about players, not coaches. A coach is only a tool in the process, and a coach should never be above the process. Coach Mayberry was not big-headed, but he was feeling pretty good about himself as a coach. When Keith went down with a broken ankle, the other players elevated their game to the max, but it wasn't enough to win the district. The lesson is simple. Remember, good players make good coaches, and when you have a good team that is winning, it is easy to forget that issue. I can't even begin to tell you how many coaches are on an ego trip because they think so much of themselves as coaches. It is human nature. In fact, it is harder to find humble coaches than ego-driven coaches in our day and time. The truth is that the players make the shots, get the rebounds, make the assists, guard the opponents and win the game. You, as a coach, can lose the game, but you seldom win the game. It takes skill and talent to win games, and how much talent you have will determine how much you can win regardless of what level of play you are coaching. Bottom line—coaching is overrated. Since I believe that coaching is overrated, my main purpose is to create talented basketball players, then teach them how to win games.

CHAPTER SIX

COACHING LESSON-ONE
WHO ARE YOU LEARNING FROM?
PERMIAN HIGH SHOOL   6A

Coach Mayberry begins his football coaching at Permian High School [Friday night lights] with eight different kinds of football coaches for him to observe and learn from. Coach Mayberry felt he had received a Master's degree in coaching football during his first spring training. Each coach was very professional and each coach knew his assignment almost to perfection. He had never witnessed the level of intensity that he was experiencing learning from those eight different coaches. The question I have for coaches is: who are you learning from? If you aren't learning, then you are going downhill.

COACHING LESSON-TWO
SURVIVAL OF THE FITTEST
PERMIAN HIGH SCHOOL   6A

Coaching at Permian, Coach Mayberry learned a different kind of dynasty in athletics. He had observed Brownwood and the dynasty they had, but at Permian High School it was different. In the Permian, it was a situation where it amounted to the survival of the fittest. It was a survival course, and the athletes that made it until they were seniors were the best. In other words, the Permian created athletes that maxed out on their talent level. Most athletes use about 60% of their talent, but at Permian, because of the program, the athletes usually max out at 90-100% of their talent level. At Permian, there was no such thing as an underachiever, and because of that, Permian created a dynasty in football.

COACHING LESSON-THREE
PLAYING HARD VS PLAYING SOFT IN BASKETBALL
PERMIAN HIGH SCHOOL   6A

Coach Mayberry had an assistant coach that didn't understand the concept of playing hard vs. playing soft in basketball. Coach Mayberry tried to explain, but it didn't register with his assistant coach. Often, football players that play basketball play basketball in a soft manner. The reason is simple. In football, the whistle blows at the end of the play and everyone has a chance to regroup. They can rethink what has happened and what they want to do next. That creates a different kind of reaction, and it takes a football player some time to change this type of behavior. Because of that, football players that play basketball are often caught standing around watching instead of reacting. In basketball there is no time to think and it depends on your background of fundamentals how you handle the transition from one skill to another skill. That is why most players look like they are non-aggressive because they are caught off guard. Football players are naturally aggressive, and it takes time to adjust to how to be aggressive in basketball. Playing hard is difficult to define, and many great coaches have attempted to do just that. My definition of playing hard is playing the game all out on both ends of the court without fear of failure.

COACHING LESSON-FOUR
NO DYNASTY WITHOUT STRONG ADMINISTRATIVE SUPPORT
PERMIAN HIGH SCHOOL   6A

Coach Mayberry is learning what makes Permian so special day by day. All coaches want to be a part of a dynasty, and all coaches want to know what makes a program a dynasty. Coach Mayberry explains why Permian wins in another way. Not only do the players in the football program max out, the coaches max out. Coaches work from dawn to sunset day after day. Permian had two teams of football scouts who are school employees that teach classes and coached during the day. On the day to scout, both groups would be on the road, doing whatever it took to scout a team that Permian was playing. The football team would work out each morning, going through preparation for the coming game. Coaches were intense and players picked up information whether they were ready or not. Preparation was a big advantage at Permian, and administrative support was evident because of the classes that coaches missed due to this kind of preparation. You can't do what Permian was doing without administrative support, and that support was critical to the success of the Permian football program.

COACHING LESSON-FIVE
COMMUNITY SUPPORT IS THE BOTTOM LINE FOR SUCCESS IN ATHLETICS ON THE HIGH SCHOOL LEVEL
PERMIAN HIGH SCHOOL   6A

Coach Mayberry accepted the challenge of presenting the football scouting report to the Permian Booster Club for the first game of the season. That ended up being the final nail on the head about why Permian had a football dynasty. The high school cafeteria seated close to 500 students, but when over 1,000 boosters crowded into the cafeteria to hear the football scouting report about the first football game at Permian, Coach Mayberry knew what made the Mojo so special. Community support is the strongest motivation a program can have. The reason is that they allow you to coach without the fear of someone looking over your shoulder. Because of that attitude, you can do what needs to be done in order to win. But there is a down side to that attitude. The morning after Permian lost a game and didn't make the playoffs, Coach Wilkins had twenty-three for sale signs in his front yard, even though Permian had won nine and lost one.

COACHING LESSON-SIX
WHAT MAKES "FRIDAY NIGHT LIGHTS" SO SPECIAL FOR ALL THE SPORTS AT PERMIAN
PERMIAN HIGH SCHOOL   6A

Coach Mayberry was always asked the question why he liked Permian since it was a strong football school. Coach Mayberry liked Permian because they had plenty of athletes to go around and Permian wanted to win in everything they did. "Friday Night Lights" was special because it brought so much excitement, fun competition, rivalry between schools, and excellent participation for the young and old. At Permian, football was number one, but it continued into basketball and other sports as well.

COACHING LESSON-SEVEN
ADAPTING TO YOUR PLAYERS ON HAND
PERMIAN HIGH SCHOOL   6A

Coach Mayberry knew he had some good young players coming. The junior varsity and sophomore teams won the district. Coach Mayberry gives us a coaching lesson. Coaches, please hear me out on this issue and think about what I am about to say. Are you a coach that the players have to adjust to, or are you a coach that can adjust to the players? The majority of successful coaches are the ones that the players have to adjust to. Some coaches, particularly at the college level, are almost mean in this particular area of coaching. Coach Mayberry had a group of young athletes, none very big, except for one young man who was not a very good athlete. In his first year, Coach Mayberry ran a highlow power game offense. He had David Nelson, who was 6'7" tall, and Darryl Hunt, at 6'5", and they were both good players. Coming up in the ranks were more guard-oriented players with decent athletic abilities. So, Coach Mayberry went to work trying to figure out what kind of offense would best suit those players. He taught his assistant coach the "McMurry offense" created by Hershel Kimbrough. The offense was a shuffle type of offense, and both the junior varsity and the sophomore team won the district championship by executing the offense. He adapted his thinking to fit the players coming up next and it proved very successful. How many of your coaches do that? From my experience, which spans almost fifty-three years, very few.

COACHING LESSON-EIGHT
PERMIAN HIGH SCHOOL   6A
ARE YOU KEEPING UP WITH THE GAME YOU ARE COACHING?

Coach Mayberry attends a basketball clinic in the spring that changes his way of thinking. Jim Reid was the main basketball speaker, and his speech was about what you should be reading as a coach to improve yourself. When Coach Mayberry thought about what he was reading, he was embarrassed. He wasn't reading much at all, and that hit him hard to the core about his coaching. Coach Mayberry was a good motivator, but he wasn't keeping up with the game like he should have, and this clinic got his attention. With the help of several books and magazines that included several big-time coaches, particularly John Wooden and Bobby Knight, Coach Mayberry started upgrading his coaching style. "Practical Modern Basketball" by John Wooden became his basketball bible. "How to Coach the Passing Game" by Bobby Knight was an old article about half-court offense and creating an offseason basketball program. Bobby Knight's book became an assistant coach for Coach Mayberry.

With new concepts and knowledge, Coach Mayberry bought weighted vests, weighted ropes, dribbling blinders, and jumping boxes and then developed an off-season basketball program for Permian High School. Then Coach Mayberry copied parts of the Permian football off-season program and installed it along with his basketball thoughts, going two times a day just like the football team. His thinking was that if the football team can do it, then we can do it. After four weeks, the players bought into the new program, and soon the results could be seen by the naked eye. He noticed pride was developing in the basketball program and confidence within each player was abundant. So, what is the lesson in this chapter? Coaches need to stay up with the game by reading, going to clinics, and watching videos, making every attempt to learn more about the game of basketball. But the real lesson in this is to open your mind to improvement and then put into play what you have learned. Most coaches do read and explore in their mind's different styles of basketball and different concepts in basketball. The problem is that all the information stays in their heads and never gets to the court. Most coaches that I know are very informative, but they enjoy living within their own comfort zone because that is safe. Being safe as a coach is not the way to grow. You don't like players that won't try things. They are always playing it safe. Playing it safe is like not participating. You wouldn't put up with that kind of attitude from a player, but yet, you, as a coach, will stay in your comfort zone rather than attempt to learn and grow as a coach. It is just a matter of time when you will find yourself getting behind other coaches, just as it is with a basketball player. Players don't stay the same because they either get better or get behind. Wake up before you start falling behind, coaches.

COACHING LESSON-NINE
PERMIAN HIGH SCHOOL   6A
COACHING IS A TWO-WAY STREET AND IT STARTS WITH YOU

All of a sudden, Coach Mayberry had the same feeling about his group at Permian that he had at Adrian, Albany, and Hereford. Coaches need to understand that coaching is a two-way street and if you want that warm fuzzy that makes you feel good about what you are doing, then you need to give more of yourself without expecting so much from the players. When you do that, good things happen between you and the players. Coaching is about the player and not you. Real relationships start with you and the effort you make toward them.

COACHING LESSON-TEN
TOUGH DECISIONS NEED TO BE BASED ON WHAT IS RIGHT FOR THE TEAM FROM THE BEST PLAYER TO THE WORST
PERMIAN HIGH SCHOOL   6A

Coach Mayberry had a star named Darryl Hunt, and he decides after football that he needs to explore his options in football, which will conflict with his playing basketball. Darryl Hunt is a big-time football prospect and he does need to use his visits to different schools to further his football career, which eventually ends up in a pro football contract. This creates a huge decision that Coach Mayberry has to make, which will decide many issues involved with Coach Mayberry's desire to build a basketball program at Permian. You are hired to be in charge and you need to make the decision regardless of the outcome, but your decision should be based on what is right for your team, not one individual, even if the team can't see what you see.

COACHING LESSON-ELEVEN
JEALOUSY BETWEEN COACHES IN DIFFERENT SPORTS CAN CREATE PROBLEMS FOR THE SCHOOL DISTRICT
PERMIAN HIGH SCHOOL   6A

COACH Mayberry is confronted by the head football coach about two players coming from junior high school that have decided not to play football the next year. The meeting was directed at Coach Mayberry, meaning that it was his fault that those two junior high players were dropping out of football. This is old hat for a boys' basketball coach because it happens everywhere in schools across the United States. Most of the time, football coaches outnumber boys' basketball coaches four to one. Intimidation is the major way a football coach attempts to get under the skin of a basketball coach. It shouldn't be part of the school system, but it is and always will be. It's the same in all sports, but the dominant sport will always have the upper hand. It could be volleyball coach vs. girls' basketball coach or girls' basketball coach vs. volleyball coach, or boys' track coach vs. boys' baseball coach. You need an objective administrator in this situation, and in Texas that just doesn't happen very often. The football coach is usually the athletic director, especially in small schools where sports have to share athletes. What is terrible in most cases is that the student athlete and their parents are caught in the middle of different coaches' ego trips. This usually ends in jealousy between the two sports and never has a good ending. That was one of the reasons why Larry Wartes was my hero. He was the best athletic director and football coach that I have ever been around, and it wasn't from his words but from his actions. He supported fairness and he supported people that were willing to work with each other instead of those that were working against each other.

COACHING LESSON-TWELVE

A GOOD COACH LEARNS TO LISTEN TO THEIR SPOUSE- BECAUSE THEY WELL TELL YOU THE TRUTH WHETHER YOU LIKE IT OR NOT

PERMIAN HIGH SCHOOL   6A

Coach Mayberry was offered a football position in Borger along with his friend Jim Breckenridge, who was going to be the Head Football

Coach. When Coach Mayberry talked to his wife, Jeany, about the move, she was not too happy with this thought. Coaches' wives are the most important asset a coach can have. Coaches should never forget that wives are in the stands and they hear all the negative voices that you never hear. Wives are the hidden partners you have in your coaching career, and they fight more battles for you than you will ever begin to fight. A good coach's wife is patient, smart, understanding, compassionate, tough-minded, nurse, has good driving skills, logical, God-loving, no ego, prophet, great management skills, and excellent phone manners. Not to mention, she needs to be a psychiatrist. The lesson in this paragraph is simple. Listen to your wife because she really cares about you and, most importantly, treat your wife like she is a queen. When your wife disagrees with you, listen; don't pout; and when your wife tells you something that you need to hear, listen; then love her for it. Of course, the same is true of a husband if the wife is a coach and he has to live with your coaching situation.

COACHING LESSON-THIRTEEN

EXPECTATIONS ARE THE KEY TO HOW YOU THINK AND THAT IS THE KEY TO WHAT YOU DO

BORGER HIGH SCHOOL   5A

Coach Mayberry and Coach Breckenridge moved to Borger to install the Permian way of football. Coach Mayberry felt good about what they were doing, but something was missing. Coach Mayberry learned another great lesson in coaching when he went to Borger to help his head coach install the Permian football system. Developing a program is a process, and it takes years for that process to take place. Senior football players at Brownwood and Permian knew what was expected of them and all wanted to lead by example, giving young players an example to follow. The senior leadership was good for Borger standards but not in our eyes because we were thinking in terms of Permian standards. The community's support was good in terms of what was expected at Borger, but compared to Permian, it was almost nothing. The athletes weren't close to what Permian had, but in Borger's eyes, they thought it was good. At Permian expectations were very high and at Borger they were very low, but Borger thought they were high. The coaches at Borger were great and wonderful coaches, but their expectations were low in terms of our expectations. We were used to the expectations at Permian and, because of that, our expectations were very high. The Borger coaches didn't have the experience of expecting the best of each player because that was the norm at Borger. The administration at Borger was great and they supported us 100%. The lesson for coaches in this paragraph is that leadership happens to be the key to change. If you aren't willing to be a leader, then don't attempt to make a change. Leadership can be lonely, so expect conflicts but demand the opportunity to win those conflicts. The bottom line for this lesson is to remember that what you expect is what you are going to get. Coaches make two huge mistakes, and I am as guilty as anyone. They expect too little of their players or they have their mind already made up by putting players in certain categories before even giving them a chance to fail or succeed. Now the real problem lies in your own evaluation of yourself. Very few, if any, can really evaluate themselves, especially coaches. Coaches are their own enemies because they get their ego and pride in the way of improvement. Are you one of those coaches? Good coaches require both pride and ego, but it is the correct balance of ego and pride that distinguishes the really good coaches from the average coach.

COACHING LESSON-FOURTEEN
GOOD STUFF HAPPENS WHEN YOU STAY THE COURSE AND FINISH THE JOB
MIDLAND JUNIOR COLLEGE   D1

Coach Mayberry receives a phone call from Chester Story, and when Coach Mayberry returns the call, Chester Story offers Coach Mayberry the **POSITION OF HEAD GOLF COACH AND ASSISTANT BASKETBALL COACH.** Since Coach Mayberry had applied before, and wasn't offered the position, Coach Mayberry asked Chester to explain. Coach Story told Coach Mayberry that now he is considered a football coach instead of a basketball coach. Coach Mayberry was a basketball coach when he applied. The board felt that was too many basketball coaches and not fair to the other sports. Fate has so much to do with your life as a coach. Don't try to manipulate it, just go with the flow and things will work out. At times you may think this is not worth it but if you will stay the course and do the job all will work out in the long run. The key is to stay the course and do the job.

COACHING LESSON-FIFTHTEEN
THINK SERIOUSLY BEFORE JUMPING INTO A COLLEGE LEVEL COACHING POSITION
MIDLAND COLLEGE   D1

Welcome to Recruiting 101. Most high school coaches think they want to be a college coach. They never see the negative side of being a college coach. What everyone doesn't see is this: lots of failure and lots of effort are the main characteristics of a good college coach in recruiting because they see more negatives than positives. Think about how you handle adversity before you want to jump into the college scene. That includes getting fired at the college level because that is a reality.

COACHING LESSON-SIXTEEN
MIDLAND COLLEGE   6A
NEVER-NEVER GET SATISFIED WITH YOUR RECRUITING IN COLLEGE

If you are a college coach, recruiting is the name of the game. When you get satisfied with your results, you are about to take a hit. Coach Mayberry had his recruiting finished and felt comfortable, then he had to learn a hard lesson. Three of his recruits decided at the last minute that they were not coming to Midland College. Coach Mayberry didn't have a backup list or any other recruits on his list, so he was caught without any prospects to contact. Later on, Coach Mayberry learned from that experience to never be without player prospects. He learned to have more than enough but, for sure, not less than enough.

COACHING LESSON-SEVENTEEN
DON'T STAY A HOME-BOY ALL YOUR LIFE-EXPAND YOUR KNOWLEDGE-GROW AS A COACH

Coach Mayberry is beginning his college experience by recruiting college basketball players. His first recruiting trips were to Kentucky, Indiana, and Illinois. Coach Mayberry has been mentored by Coach Story and believes that recruiting is the heart of winning. When Coach Mayberry arrives in the state requested by Coach Story, he learns something that he never knew before. The basketball mentality, basketball intelligence, and basketball IQ over- all were superior to Texas. Not only that, the overall play of the individual basketball players was far better than any he had seen in Texas. He had talented players, but something was different in these states, and he couldn't put it down on paper, but he could see the difference. Coach Mayberry was watching high-class basketball players play, but they didn't act in the same manner that the really good players in Texas acted. They had more class and composure. That goes with expectations, and in Kentucky, Illinois, and Indiana, expectations were high. Not only that the better athletes played basketball in these states where in Texas the better athletes play football. It was a totally different mentality, and he loved it. What happened in this experience was something that carried him over his entire career in college coaching. The world is big and unless you don't explore it, then you will remain a home boy without the experience of knowing any difference. Explore for growth, if not for anything else.

COACHING LESSON-EIGHTEEN
MIDLAND COLLEGE 6A
EVERY COACH REGARLESS OF WHAT LEVEL OF PLAY NEEDS A PLAN ON HOW TO HANDLE OFFICIALS

Official's will read this and think Chester Story had a terrible attitude towards basketball officials. That thinking would be just the opposite of how he really feels about basketball officials. Chester preaches to his players on a day-to-day basis about respect for the officials, and even before the game starts, he always gives a speech about being able to accept the authority of the officials calling the game. It was never disrespect, but Chester was very competitive, and when a competitive coach gets in the heat of the battle, often he will be misrepresentative by his actions in a game. The lesson is simple. If you are going to coach, you need to develop an attitude about how to handle the game officials. You must Work at it just like you work at all the other details of coaching. It must be something that you remind yourself of daily, and especially before a game. Develop a plan and then go by that plan.

CHAPTER SEVEN

COACHING LESSON-ONE
IF YOU WANT TO LEARN-ASK AND YOU WILL RECEIVE

Coach Mayberry needs advice on recruiting, so he calls two successful college coaches, Mike Mitchell at Western Texas Junior College and Gerald Myers at Texas Tech University. With the help of those two coaches, Coach Mayberry started his first recruiting class at Odessa College using the information they provided him on the phone. Don't be so prideful that you won't ask for help.

COACHING LESSON-TWO
HOW TO CHANGE A PROGRAM ATTITUDE

Coach Mayberry went to the heads of all the departments at Odessa College in an attempt to find out what was wrong with the Odessa College basketball program. When he finally gets the information he needs, he goes to work. If there is a will, there is a way. Do what you are hired to do, don't look back, get their attention and do what it takes. That is the key to turning a bad program into a good one. You can't do it worrying about what everyone thinks, but only about what you know you have to do. Do it.

COACHING LESSON-THREE
STYLE OF PLAY

When Western Texas University won the National NCAA championship in 1966, Coach Mayberry decided that he wanted to coach the same way Don Haskins coached. Don Haskins was a huge Hank Iba believer, and so was Coach Mayberry. His influence came from high school when he was coached by Gib Ford, an All American at Oklahoma State University, where Hank Iba became a legend in coaching basketball. Coach Mayberry was a huge fan of the Boston Celtics, particularly Bill Russell and Bob Cousey. A coach needs to understand that the style of play will determine success or failure many more times than a lack of talent. When determining what kind of play you want to coach, you need to consider many factors. I have seen almost any style, so I can't honestly say that one style isn't always better than the other, but I feel you must suit your style to the players you have to work with on a daily basis. Don't put your players in a style that they can't play or, more importantly, win. The next thing to consider is if your style of play allows your players to develop to their maximum ability level. One of the most important aspects of the style of play is transition basketball, offensively and defensively. When someone mentions transition, we always think of fast break offense, and although that is a big part of transition, it isn't the entire part of transition. Transition is not just going from offense to defense or defense to offense, but change. That can happen on the offensive end when a player has the ball and passes it to his teammate, who now has the ball. The player that passed the ball is now a player without the ball, and his role changes, which is another form of transition. The kind of teams you have to play and the school tradition have a lot to do with the style of play. There is no perfect style of play because all styles have weaknesses and strengths. Decide what you feel you can coach and then start learning all you can about coaching your style of play and you will be successful. Just remember that the players playing the game are what make your style work, so be sure and give them the credit.

COACHING LESSON-FOUR
EVERYONE DESERVES THE OPPORTUNTITY TO FAIL

During my time coaching in the college arena, the biggest shock for me being a yellow bird was the prejudiced attitude that so many higher-up bluebird college educators have towards black athletes. Instead of encouragement and enthusiasm about their educational opportunities, black athletes were classified into one category, just like I was in the second grade in 1946. Dumb and dumber is the word and it is still going on in our educational system TODAY. To me, there is no excuse for this attitude, particularly in a leadership role in the educational arena. If I hadn't been a yellow bird, which meant I could identify with this environment, the players I recruited to Odessa College would have never achieved anything. I was the lucky one because I could identify and then, with a chip on my shoulder, attempt to make it right. Here is the problem, and I really don't have a solution, but I know the problem. Because of their test scores, educators have a bad habit of putting yellow BIRD children in a category labeled "poor learners" because of their test scores. Test scores are a good indicator concerning most students, but not yellow birds. Because we stereo-type the yellow birds as slow learners, we destroy their desire and motivation, which happens to be what they must have in order to achieve academically. The same is true in the athletic arena. Particularly controlling types of coaches have a bad habit of making up their minds about certain players and never really giving them a chance because they already have their mind made up.

They simply believe that a talented player can't do what they are doing, even when the player is having success. But when a talented blue bird does something good, then that same coach is thinking, yes, I was right about this player. Give a person a chance to fail, and if they fail, do something about it, but don't shut them out before they fail. The heart is the strongest asset a human has and one should never underestimate the strength of the heart.

COACHING LESSON-FIVE
BE AGGRESSIVE WHEN YOU GET THE CHANCE BUT REMAIN HUMBLE

Coach Mayberry has the opportunity to tell it like it is to his COLLEGE President because he is trying to keep Coach Mayberry on board at Odessa College. Coach Mayberry has been offered the same position at Midland College. You don't get many opportunities like this in your life, so when you do, be aggressive, lay it out, so they can hear and listen to what you want. You will regret anything you miss for the rest of your life, so be clear and don't hold back.

COACHING LESSON-SIX
DON'T JUDGE A BOOK BY ITS COVER

Coach Mayberry learns a huge lesson in recruiting. The same lesson he just learned in the above lesson, but applying it to a different situation. One of the best players Coach Mayberry ever recruited was a young man who almost everyone within a hundred- mile radius thought had a bad attitude. Even Coach Mayberry thought he had a bad attitude, but when he looked into the situation, Coach Mayberry found out that his bad attitude depended on the individual perspective making the evaluation. When he did his research on the player, Coach Mayberry found out that many people thought he had a great attitude, particularly teachers and administrators. What Coach Mayberry learned is that you can't judge a book by its cover.

COACHING LESSON-SEVEN
IF YOU SAY IT-YOU BETTER DO IT

Dennis Johnson from Milby High School was one of Coach Mayberry's finest recruits, but Dennis was not doing well in his classes. From Coach Mayberry's viewpoint, it was not about ability but effort. A statement was made by Coach Mayberry that he would send Dennis home if it didn't improve. When you make a statement to a player on your team in a negative way, you better follow up or you are going to suffer. Try never to put yourself in that position, but when you do make a strong statement, particularly about discipline, you must follow through or you will lose big time and most likely never know it. Above all, you must be a coach of your word. If you say something, then follow it up and do it. In this story, Odessa College did their part, Coach Mayberry did his part, and Dennis Johnson did his part. That is what success is all about.

COACHING LESSON-EIGHT
KNOW YOUR STYLE IN RECRUITING-THEN STICK TO IT

Coach Mayberry developed a recruiting philosophy where he involved his returning players in the process. It was a fine line that was often difficult, but for Coach Mayberry, it worked very well. It not only helped him in recruiting, but it helped him gain a better understanding of his players returning.

COACHING LESSON-NINE
IT'S ALL IN HOW YOU THINK

Great players teach coaches more than coaches teach great players. Coach Mayberry was the lucky one when he recruited Craig Ehlo at Odessa College, who played fourteen years in the NBA. People always ask Coach Mayberry about what it was like to coach Craig Ehlo, and Coach Mayberry responds. The biggest thing that Craig taught me is the way he played the game. He played all out with his mind and heart in an unselfish way. Too many players play the game with one of those missing factors. It is rare in our time today to find that kind of player because the game has become so individually geared. Still, the great ones come to the top regardless because their mind is hooked to the heart, which enables the player to respond correctly for the good of the team. Craig taught me to find unselfish players that play the game with their heart and mind, then championships will follow.

COACHING LESSON-TEN
PLAYING NOT TO GET BEAT

Coach Mayberry finished up the year after four years at Odessa College with the best team in the history of Odessa College. With all that success, we were beaten in the first round of the regional play-offs. Coach Mayberry felt empty inside and felt he had let his team down with his coaching philosophy. He was too conservative and, although he did a good job of coaching, his style created a pattern of playing not to get beat instead of playing to win. Conservative coaching is a fine line between playing to win and playing not to get beat. If you are a control coach and most coaches know who they are, then you must work extra hard to not fall into the trap of playing not to get beat.

COACHING LESSON-ELEVEN
IT'S IMPOSSIBLEE FOR A PROBLEM TO BE SOLVED BY THE SAME PEOPLE THAT CREATED THE PROBLEM

When hired in a new situation, Coach Mayberry always tries to figure out why the basketball program is broke, before ever attempting to fix the issues that need to be fixed. The main philosophy to keep in mind when determining what is wrong - always remember that a good rule of thumb is that the same people that created the problem can't fix the problem. That means listening with wisdom because they are usually part of the problem. Next, understand that change has to occur in the past, but don't jump to change without studying what has been done in the past, because that will tell you what is wrong. Remember that doing the same old thing year after year and expecting different results is generally the problem. Develop a plan, get a chip on your shoulder, go to work.

COACHING LESSON-TWELVE
ALWAYS GIVE YOURSELF TWENTY-FOUR HOURS BEFORE YOU REPOND TO AN EMOTIONAL SITUATION THAT IS STRESSFUL

Coach Mayberry eliminated a player from the Wayland basketball team when he became the head coach. He made a huge mistake in the process, one that all educators should never make. Coach Mayberry wrote an emotional letter to the eliminated player explaining why he was being eliminated. The player had violated a major rule and Coach Mayberry found out by accident. When he wrote the letter, he was in a state of anger and didn't check for grammar or spelling mistakes. Soon, a copy of that letter was in the hands of all administrators and all professors at Wayland Baptist University. All the errors in the letter were in red marks. Always wait at least twenty-four hours before you react to a negative situation, particularly one that gets your hair running straight in the air. Coach Mayberry should have waited until he was in his office before writing the letter, then double checked for grammar and spelling mistakes, used Wayland Baptist University stationary, and had it cosigned by his superior. He wouldn't have had this problem if he had followed this procedure.

COACHING LESSON-THIRTEEN
WINNING AT WAYLAND BAPTIST UNIVERSITY -ON THE ROAD

Coach Mayberry explains his approach to trying to win games on the road while attempting to change the program at Wayland Baptist University. Each coach has to decide if they are playing to win or to look good while losing. It is not that hard to attempt to win if you will work at your situation and develop a game plan for winning. But you must be willing to change and be a leader, taking the responsibility for the team's success. Instead of throwing losing back on your players by saying we just don't have the talent, go compete. You must learn something new and attempt to become a different kind of coach when you are going into the battlefield without weapons. Try something different, give it a real shot, then you will be surprised how that will change your players' attitude and your attitude about your situation. Making history is hard but worth the effort The rewards are awesome when you meet a challenge head on as a coach. For the first time in the history of the school, Wayland was ranked #1 in the Dunkel ratings. History was being made.

COACHING LESSON-FOURTEEN
PROFESSIONALISM IS A TWO-WAY STREET

Coach Mayberry explains to his superior administrator that he is interviewing for a basketball position at a higher level than Wayland Baptist. Professional behavior in administrators is just as important as professional behavior in the faculty or coaches. The first time Coach Mayberry told his superior administrator he was interviewing for a better position, the attitude was good, but the second time the attitude was totally different. Instead of being excited for Coach Mayberry and proud of him his superior administrator made him feel he was being a traitor interviewing for a position that would elevate him to a higher level of professional coaching, including everything that is involved in coaching. There was no comparison between Sam Houston State University and Wayland Baptist University athletically. Sam Houston State University officials called Wayland Administration and explained that Sam Houston State University wanted to offer Ron Mayberry the head men's basketball position and were giving them a courtesy call to let them know what was happening. The President of Wayland Baptist University, went off on the phone and threatened a law suit against Sam Houston State University. The results were that Sam Houston State University backed off from offering the basketball position to Ron Mayberry. The President at Wayland was proud of his actions and told Coach Mayberry that God wanted Ron at Wayland. Now tell me, administrators, how professional is that?

COACHING LESSON-FIFTHTEEN
DON'T MESS WITH CHEMISTRY

Coach Mayberry had a team coming back that was not very talented but had great chemistry. In an attempt to create more talent, Coach Mayberry destroyed the chemistry. What is chemistry on a basketball team? That is hard to define, but you can see it when you have it. The main lesson I have for coaches is that when they do have it, don't mess with it. Chemistry in basketball is very hard to find because of the selfish nature of the game of basketball. In my fifty-three years as a coach, I remember having it about four or five times. I had a team at Wayland that had great chemistry, but I felt we needed more talent and recruited more talent. That talent destroyed the chemistry of the team. When you have players that know who the leader is on the team, you have a chance for chemistry if that player is good. When you have a team that doesn't care who scores the points, doesn't care who gets their name in the paper, and just wants to win, then you've got chemistry. It is all about winning, and when you have players that are willing to do what it takes to win without being jealous of each other, you have a chance for chemistry. Why is this important? When you have chemistry, you can win games people don't think you can win. In high school, the main enemy of chemistry is the parents, not the players on the team. Parents want their fair share of glory for their children. It is normal and understandable. The problem is when parents influence their children to behave in a negative way toward team play because they think their child doesn't get the recognition they deserve. That destroys team chemistry, and that is why team chemistry is so hard to obtain in high school. In college, the enemy is the player's ego.

COACHING LESSON-SIXTEEN
WHO IS IN CHARGE?

Coach Mayberry has an opportunity to eliminate the problem player that is creating negative situations in practice and team meetings. Coach Mayberry made the same mistake that many coaches make, and that is, he forgot who was in charge. He let his captains talk him out of eliminating a certain player when he knew that player was not what the team needed. His gut feelings had always been right and he could see the difference in his team from the negative attitude coming from one player. He backed down when his captains approached him, defending the attitude of the negative player, saying that Coach Mayberry didn't understand him and needed to give him a chance. Coach Mayberry made a huge mistake, one that many coaches make. Coach Mayberry had the experience and he had the success backed up by the many gut choices he had made. But he did not stand up to his own values and lowered them by listening to his captains instead of his gut. It was not the captain's fault because they lived in a different environment, a different age group, and a different value system. You couldn't expect anything less from them. You are the coach and you are in charge. You must make the decisions regardless of the outcome. It is your job.

COACHING LESSON-SEVENTEEN
WHAT EVERY COLLEGE COACH MUST FACE SOONER OR LATER

Coach Mayberry finally gets frustrated with having a really good team but not good enough to win a big game. Every coach must consider their strengths and weaknesses if they want more from coaching in terms of wins. Coach Mayberry was a conservative coach because that fit his personality. He was a fundamental coach with a strong fundamental defensive background and believed in doing things right in terms of character and integrity. His recruitment was similar to his personality and because he felt that he could coach that type of player. Up to this point in time in his career, Coach Mayberry had coached four blue-chip players and he felt he only had success with one of them. He didn't feel good about the other three and felt he couldn't coach them. What made it worse was deep inside him he felt responsible for his attitude about his failure with the other three blue chip players. However, coach Mayberry figured the reason for his teams' being good but not good enough was always the same. He simply didn't recruit the level of talent that was needed to win at a higher level of play. That was a hard pill for him to swallow. His pride and ego took a huge hit. Then, with the help of two of his Kilgore basketball players, Byron Hogan's and Randy Smith's, Coach Mayberry overcame his fear of coaching talented basketball players. Again, he was the lucky one.

COACHING LESSON-EIGHTEEN
WHY DRUG TEST IN COLLEGE

Coach Mayberry hears about a drug testing program at Arkansas University, then travels to the university and learns about the program. He buys into it hook, line, and sinker. Then the coach takes the program back to Kilgore College, presents the program t to the Kilgore College President, and he says no. Coach Mayberry is told that he is by himself and if anything goes wrong with his drug testing program, he will be fired. Coach Mayberry takes the challenge on by himself, including the expenses. Sometimes you, as a coach, have to stand your ground and fight for what you think is right. If you aren't willing to do that, then you should find another occupation because that is what coaching is all about. Together, Coach Mayberry and his players recruited the most successful blue-chip players available in the Southern States of the USA. Now he was making his first statement to his players that drug testing would be used and everyone knew this ahead of time. Without the help of any administration because they signed off on the issue, Coach Mayberry created a drug testing program at Kilgore College. Coach Mayberry paid for the program out of his own pocket and did all the work without any help from the administration at Kilgore College. Three young men failed the test, and two of them left the program. They didn't want their parents to know, so they left, and the other young man went through the process required and passed the next drug test. Later on, he played at New Mexico University and then went to the NBA. The concept behind drug testing is to "give players a reason to say no to drugs." Peer pressure is the number one reason for drug usage, and if you can eliminate peer pressure, your battle is half over in the fight against drug use and abuse.

COACHING LESSON-NINETEEN
STICK TO YOUR GUNS-STAY THE COURSE

Kilgore College vs. Tyler College is a huge rivalry between two towns and colleges. Twenty-five miles separate the two cities, and any kind of competition is a rivalry. Gerald Paddio missed a pregame shootaround before the big game vs. Tyler College. Coach Mayberry talked to his captains and they revealed that Gerald was getting out of hand and had a bad case of the "big head." Gerald was being recruited by almost every university basketball program in the USA and his press clippings were outstanding. It was clear to Coach Mayberry what needed to be done. Coach Mayberry had learned through experience dealing with Blue Chip players that the only way to really get their attention was to make them sit on the bench and not play them. He had done all the other stuff, and it just doesn't work with blue-chip players. Coach Mayberry knew what he needed to do. The problem was that the president of the booster club threatened Coach Mayberry. He told Coach Mayberry that he needed to find another way to discipline Gerald because we need to win this game with Tyler. In the same sentence, he hinted that they could look for someone else to coach at Kilgore if Tyler Junior College wins. Kilgore won, and what made the victory better was that some of the players stepped up their game and played above what they had been playing. Gerald saw what was happening and after the game in the dressing room, humbled himself with an apology to the players on the team. After that, Kilgore College was very hard to beat, and had they not lost Bryon Hogans to a knee injury, they would have won the National Championship. The lesson here is for coaches not to be afraid to discipline their best players. Most of the time, your players already know when a player needs some discipline, and when you administer the discipline, you will gain their respect. It's when you don't discipline the best player that you lose respect from the team.

COACHING LESSON-TWENTY
BE LOYAL TO YOUR COMMITMENT

Coach Mayberry made a verbal commitment to accept the head basketball position at South Plains College a week before the season ended. After the last game at Kilgore, he was asked by the Athletic Director of the University of Texas at San Antonio if he would be interested in visiting with him about the Head Basketball position. Coach Mayberry told them that he had already committed to South Plains College in Levelland, Texas. There is no comparison between the two schools because one is a division one NCAA school and the other is a division one NJCAA school. Nothing is close, and Coach Mayberry says no to a visit. Character and integrity are two parts of being a coach. Neither is something that you will get hired for, but both are something that makes you the person that you are. Coaching needs both qualities, and only you know if you have them. After fifty-three years in the business of coaching, I am proud of the fact that I was loyal to my word, but I can see the other side of the coin and often wonder what life would have given me if I chose the other. Regardless of my thinking, my family turned out the way I thought it would, so how can I second guess that? It all depends on what is important to you. Have you really been challenged? I will never forget the Athletic Director words when I told him that I was going to South Plains College. He said, " I am glad that I found out about you because I certainly made a mistake about you thinking you could be our head basketball coach."

CHAPTER EIGHT

COACHING LESSON-ONE
A PRESIDENT WITH INTEGRITY AND CHARACTER
SOUTH PLAINS JUNIOR COLLEGE   D1

Coach Mayberry interviews with Dr. Baker, the President of South Plains College. Dr. Baker was just what Coach Mayberry was looking for in a president. He was strong in every area that existed at SPC. He took pride in all the programs at SPC and admitted that the men's basketball program was one of his failures, but he was handing that task over to the Athletic Director, Joe Tubb. He said that he wanted to win but wasn't willing to cheat to win, and told me that he would work hard to help us turn the table in men's basketball.

COACHING LESSON-TWO
STANDING UP FOR WHAT IS RIGHT FOR ALL CONCERNED-THAT IS WHAT A LEADER IS ALL ABOUT
SOUTH PLAINS JUNIOR COLLEGE   D1

When I presented the drug program to Dr. Baker, he not only bought into the program but demanded that all the athletes at South Plains College get drug tested. What a difference a good administrator can make to the athletes of that school. He walked the walk because his interest was in the entire group, not just the basketball group. Bottom line, he stood up for what was right.

COACHING LESSON-THREE

HAVE YOU ALREADY MADE UP YOUR MIND-WE ARE CONTROL FREAKS

SOUTH PLAINS JUNIOR COLLEGE   D1

Coach Mayberry didn't allow walk-ons at South Plains College. He had many reasons, but Robby Garner taught him all his reasons were wrong. Coach Mayberry had developed a philosophy that it was a waste of time to allow walk-ons the opportunity to play college basketball at South Plains College. Simply put, walk-on players were no match for Coach Mayberry's recruited players. The end result was usually a frustrated walk-on and a waste of time for Coach Mayberry. Then Robby Garner was given a walk-on chance, and to Coach Mayberry's surprise, Robby made an impact on the team. Coach Mayberry had fallen into the trap of making up his mind before ever giving a kid a chance. That is the major sin coaches commit. How many times do you say to yourself "that kid can't play"? Yes, you do have your reasons and yes, most of the time you are right, but when you don't give that kid a chance, then who are you cheating? Yes, even if you give that kid a chance and he doesn't make the team, he will still blame you. That is a given, but it still remains the same and that attitude will become even more dominant the longer you coach. Before long, you will be making judgments about a player before he even steps on the court. Learn to give a kid a chance to fail before you make them into a failure.

COACHING LESSON-FOUR
WHEN IT COMES TO DISCIPLINE-TREAT YOUR PLAYERS LIKE FAMILY
SOUTH PLAINS JUNIOR COLLEGE   D1

Coach Mayberry's team laid an egg in a tournament. It was simple enough because the team lacked effort. When a coach has a lack of effort, then it is time to get the attention of the players at their expense. I believe that a coach needs to approach their team just like family. If you have a son or daughter that is not giving their best effort in the classroom by not doing assignments, you must confront your child and action is required on your part. Explain why their action is not acceptable and then do something to remind them that their action is not acceptable. Discipline is required and if the discipline is a spanking, which would be the last resort, then do it right so they remember. That was the way I felt when my team didn't give the effort it took to win. We met early the next morning and ran. Then we looked at the video, and I showed them what I was talking about. Then we met again the next morning and ran. The first morning was about discipline for lack of effort. The film meeting was about explaining and showing them what I was talking about. The second straight morning run was about them remembering what we just went over.

COACHING LESSON-FIVE
HOW TO STOP A TEAM FROM SELF DESTRUCTION
SOUTH PLAINS JUNIOR COLLEGE   D1

Coach Mayberry was having problems with his team arguing and bitching at each other. Self-destruction was in front of his face because of immature attitudes. Coach Mayberry and Coach Lloyd decided to teach the guys on the team a lesson about being positive instead of negative regarding teammates. In the middle of practice, Coach Mayberry and Coach Lloyd started an argument, having a strong confrontation with each other in front of the players. Both Coach Mayberry and Coach Lloyd made negative comments towards each other, then walked off the court, leaving practice. The players on the court became divided, with some going after Coach Mayberry and some after Coach Lloyd. When both coaches reached the top level of the stairs, they turned around and came back to the court. It was then that Coach Mayberry and Coach Lloyd explained that they were play-acting, showing the players an example of how they had been acting. All of a sudden, they understood how both coaches felt when they acted in such a negative manner. For the first time, they understood how stupid they looked. We never had a similar problem like that the rest of the year.

COACHING LESSON-SIX

A GOOD LEADER PROJECTS SUPPORT AND CONFIDENCE
SOUTH PLAINS JUNIOR COLLEGE

Dr. Baker [**THE PRESIDENT OF SOUTH PLAINS COLLEGE**] sat right behind the home team during games. Some coaches might feel pressured by that action, but that was not the case with Coach Mayberry. I wanted to win as badly as Dr. Baker wanted us to win, so I never felt uneasy about him sitting directly behind our bench but rather liked it. He wanted to win as badly as anyone, and he was footing the bill. I wanted to win for him as much as for the other players on the team. A good administrator gives a coach confidence along with support instead of fear.

COACHING LESSON-SEVEN
DO YOU KNOW THE TECHIQUE
SOUTH PLAINS JUNIOR COLLEGE   D1

Coach Mayberry was selected to give a clinic to basketball coaches throughout the Canary Islands. Every night he would meet with coaches and give a clinic about basketball. Coach Mayberry learned that he didn't understand Technique like he should because that was the main issue the coaches were concerned about. Coaches in the Canary Islands were more interested in the proper footwork for passing, catching, shooting, and receiving the basketball. Also, they needed information on footwork on defense, pivoting, and rebounding. The clinic taught Coach Mayberry one thing. He didn't really know technique as much as he should have. Do you?

COACHING LESSON-EIGHT
NUMBER ONE RULE COACH-MAKE TIME FOR YOUR FAMILY
SOUTH PLAINS JUNIOR COLLEGE   D1

Coach Mayberry was having a difficult time keeping up with his family because of conflicting work, making it difficult to be a good father and husband. So, he declared Sunday night a night where they would have a family team meeting. No outside influence of any kind would be allowed during this time period. If there is a lesson, I can put emphasis on, it would be this one. Simply put, make time for your family and remember your promises. The hardest thing for a coach is learning to keep promises instead of making them.

COACHING LESSON-NINE
HOW DO YOU COUNTER CHEATING IN RECRUITMENT?
SOUTH PLAINS JUNIOR COLLEGE   D1

Coach Mayberry and Eddie Fields are in a recruiting battle with several colleges, who is from the Baton Rouge area. Money is being offered for Keith to sign with some other schools, and Coach Mayberry tells Eddie Fields to top that offer. Coach Mayberry told Eddie to tell Keith's mother that we would make sure Keith got an education with a chance to get a degree. Coach Mayberry told Eddie to tell his mom that we were going to make him go to class, make him go to study-hall, and make him do his school work. We would stay on top of his studies like he was our own son and if he gets out of line one inch, she will be notified. His education is more important to us than anything we can do. The lesson here is simple. A student's education is the most important issue facing young people today. It is our job as coaches to help students in every possible way necessary to get the job done in the academic arena. Everything else is secondary. Eddie did sign Keith.

COACHING LESSON-TEN
CHARACTER IS DOING WHAT IS RIGHT WHEN EVERYONE THINKS WHAT YOU ARE DOING IS WRONG
SOUTH PLAINS JUNIOR COLLEGE   D1

In the regional tournament, South Plains College was defeated by a team they had beaten twice before. Preparation was poor on both parts, and it showed during the game. SPC lost, and now they had to travel back to Levelland on the same day since the game was played at noon. Sometimes, as a leader, you must make hard decisions that will leave lasting impressions on everyone involved in your program. Sending the players home instead of letting them stay overnight was a tough choice, but one that was needed because it makes a statement to all concerned. One, it was a school rule, and two, it reminds them that they are still part of a school environment even though they are 400 miles away from their school. The school is paying the expenses, and they are still part of the school that they represent.

COACHING LESSON-TEN
BE PREPARED FOR THE UNEXPECTED IN RECRUITING SOUTH PLAINS JUNIOR COLLEGE   D1

Coach Mayberry was recruiting Bo Outlaw, who ended up playing in the NBA for thirteen years. At the time of this writing, Bo was working for the Orlando Magic in the administrative offices. Bo had made a commitment to sign with South Plains College, but when coach Mayberry called to reaffirm his commitment, there was no answer on the phone. After calling several times and getting no answer, Coach Mayberry knew he had a problem. Coach Mayberry's gut instinct told him something was wrong, so he went to San Antonio that day. When you are recruiting, the first rule to remember is that your timetable is on the recruit's timetable and not yours. The second lesson you learn is that your job is never done until that recruit signs on the dotted line. Of course, that is when your real job begins, but first you must do your homework and make sure you cover all your basic people that are involved with the recruit. Recruiting is never easy, and you should always expect the unexpected and be prepared. Had I not had resources on hand to convince the proper people, we wouldn't have signed Bo Outlaw? Be determined and always listen to your gut because 95% of the time it will be right. In my case, it is 99%.

COACHING LESSON-ELEVEN
ITS ONE THING TO GET TO THE TOP BUT ANOTHER TO STAY AT THE TOP
SOUTH PLAINS JUNIOR COLLEGE   D1

Coach Mayberry had finally turned the program around at South Plains College. Now everyone was shooting at South Plains. Coach Mayberry understood the saying about "It's one thing to get to the top, but another to stay at the top". Your work only begins when you get to the top, and then your consistency is even more important and your decisions are game breakers. Always remember to stay humble because everyone will be learning from you.

COACHING LESSON-TWELVE
TOO MUCH ATTENTION DESTROYS NOT BUILDS
SOUTH PLAINS JUNIOR COLLEGE   D1

Too much attention destroys not builds Coach Mayberry attempted to control college scouts' contact with his players. But their contact with scouts was a constant battle, with scouts calling at night, scouts coming to the gym to watch them play, and scouts sending players letters, e-mails, and other information about their school. It was a no-win situation. Coach Mayberry learned that too much attention to specific players can be very negative in terms of achievement and performance for the players getting the attention. Some of his players started playing for someone else instead of South Plains College. That kind of thinking leads to poor play, and the end result is always the same. Scouts would back off specific players they were recruiting, but the truth happened to be that the scouts created the problem to begin with. Because the bottom line in this situation is that the recruit ends up losing, coach Mayberry developed a strong attitude toward the rules the scouts had to follow and, because of that, he was often misunderstood. Don't get so involved in the process of recruiting that you forget the reason you are coaching. You want players to be the best they can be, and when something interferes in that process, you, as a coach, need to step up as a leader and do what is right.

COACHING LESSON-THIRTEEN

CHEMISTRY ON THE TEAM IS THE ANSWER IF YOU CAN UNDERSTAND IT

SOUTH PLAINS JUNIOR COLLEGE   D1

Coach Mayberry had a team that was considered the best team ever in the history of South Plains College and finished with a record of thirty-two wins and two losses, which at that time was the best ever. Poor chemistry on a team will destroy your team regardless of what you do as a coach, and most of the time, poor chemistry leads to destruction. The above record tells you how good we really were because we had poor chemistry we did not advance to the National Tournament. The following season, the 1991-92 season, Coach Mayberry coached a team that won the regional tournament, then went to the national tournament and finished with four wins and one loss for fifth place in the national junior college basketball tournament. The only loss was a double overtime loss to the team that won the national junior college tournament. Everything was totally different in the playoffs as Coach Mayberry's team played their best basketball of the year. Before the regional tournament, very few recruiters visited SPC and the interest in the players playing at the Division One level was void. At the end of the regional and national tournaments, almost everyone on the team was being recruited. The year before, during the 1990-91 basketball season, Coach Mayberry never had a practice that didn't have a handfull of Division One recruiters watching practice. Coach Mayberry had two guys that transferred to Arkansas [Cory Beck and Dwight Stewart] that eventually won the National NCAA tournament their junior year and finished second their senior year. Two other guys [Bo Outlaw and David Diaz] played for the University of Houston and led them to the Southwest Conference Championship. Later, Bo Outlaw played in the NBA for thirteen years, and David Diaz played professional basketball in Venezuela for many years. In each of the Olympics, David Diaz played on the Venezuela Olympic basketball team. Two other players [Terry Alexander and Artie Griffin] on that 1990-91 team played Division One basketball and both played NBA basketball. The 1990-91 team played horrible basketball at the regional tournament, losing in the regional finals. What was the difference? Chemistry is the answer. Chemistry on a team is hard to define because it comes in different forms, but when you have it, you will know it. It always comes when you have excellent leadership. You can't define it or control it, but it just happens when you least expect it. I have seen many coaches try to control it only to fail. Second, you must have players willing to sacrifice for the good of the team. Third, you must have players that can perform under pressure on a consistent basis, especially the go-to players on offense. Fourth, you must have individual players that feel a strong responsibility toward each other in regards to effort on the court on both ends of the court.

COACHING LESSON-FOURTEEN
THE BURGER KING MIRACLE-CHEMISTRY CAN BE LUCK
SOUTH PLAINS COLLEGE   D1

Coach Mayberry is facing the same situation again with his team. No chemistry, but instead several individuals with different agendas. Then a miracle happened. Coach Mayberry calls that miracle the Burger King Miracle, which turns the team around and they go on to win twelve of fourteen games, finishing fifth in the nation. Before the miracle happened, SPC was on a downer losing several games in a row, and looking like they were not going to make the play-offs. Then one night two of the Players on the team got into a fight in the dorm over a Burger King Hamburger. What had happened was that one of the players [player A] gave another player [player B] some money to go buy a Hamburger for him at a Burger King. When [player B] got back to the dorm, he had eaten the Burger instead of bringing it back to [player A]. Then player A] and [player B] got into a fight. Long story short, [player B] was kicked out of school. [Player B] had been in trouble many times before. [Player A] had never been in trouble. [Player B] was a problem player on the team and when he left, the team started winning again. Matter of fact, they turned everything around winning the regional championship. There are two huge lessons in these paragraphs. The first lesson is to never give up on your team. Two, work at creating the proper chemistry on your team. You can't control it, but if you work at it, you have a better chance of getting good chemistry instead of poor chemistry.

COACHING LESSON-FIFTHTEEN
THE STRONGEST FACTOR TOWARD WINNING-COMMITMENT TO THE TEAM
SOUTH PLAINS JUNIOR COLLEGE   D1

Coach Mayberry's team at South Plains College struggled with many problems in his last year at SPC. Because of that, the team had a hard time buying into each other and him as a coach. It was a very difficult year for Coach Mayberry and his team. They were playing the last game, and with a win they could make the regional tournament. However, they were playing the conference champion at their place. It was Howard College, and they had eight Division One signees. South Plains didn't have one player being recruited at that time of the year. Coach Mayberry told the team that they could play the game his way and have a chance to win, or play the game their way and get defeated by twenty points or more. The team decided to commit to Coach Mayberry's coaching, then went to Howard and defeated them by one point. Coach Mayberry calls it the greatest upset in his coaching career, which spans fifty-three years. You might ask yourself what was the difference that allowed the team to have a chance to win. Simple—they committed to playing together and focused on playing as a team. They bought into Coach Mayberry's style in order to win, but the biggest difference was that Howard College had already won the game before the game was played.

COACHING LESSON-SIXTEEN
POOR LEADER VS. GOOD LEADER-YOU DECIDE
SOUTH PLAINS JUNIOR COLLEGE   D1

After coaching at South Plains College, Mr. Mayberry was moved into administration as the Dean of Men at South Plains College. The college cafeteria was struggling financially because of a lack of students eating in the cafeteria. Mr. Mayberry had a plan that he thought would fill the dorms, which would in turn fill the cafeteria. Mr. Mayberry took his plan to the President of the College. Dr. Baker was the President of the College, and he listened to Mr. Mayberry's plan with an open mind. That is the difference between a good administrator and a poor administrator. A good administrator listens with an open mind, not a closed mind, and then considers all parties involved before any decisions are made. Poor administrators make up their mind the minute the presentation is made because they already see too many problems. In other words, they do the same thing coaches do by saying it won't work because of this or that and just making excuses for it never working. It is the same thing a coach does when they already have their mind made up that a player can't do something without even giving that player a chance to prove the coach right or wrong. The number one rule for any administrator is to learn to listen with an open mind.

COACHING LESSON-SEVENTEEN
WINNING-WHAT IS WINNING?
TRINITY CHRISTIAN SCHOOLS

Coach Mayberry was hired as the Athletic Director/Head Boys Basketball Coach at Trinity Christian Schools. He was hired to mentor all coaches in all the sports about what athletics was about. Secondly, he was hired to teach the athletes what a good sports program was about and finally, to teach the parents within the school program what athletics was all about. Coach Mayberry had a huge job on his hand because Trinity was basically a participation school where winning was put on the back burner and participation was more important. That way, every child was a winner and had a trophy. Winning is something that very few people really understand. Winning is a journey, and hopefully a journey where you grow as an individual in every way you can grow. Winning is trying, and the other is losing. A person that tries with everything they have is a winner regardless of the outcome, and that is what sports are about. Team sports create an atmosphere that demands a covenant between coach, player, and teammates that enables mutual accountability and encouragement. In that process of working together to be the best they can you develop into a winner regardless of the outcome of the game There are no losers in the process of trying to be the best you can be, unless you cheat during the process. A covenant between hard work and a common goal builds character and gains power within each individual involved.

COACHING LESSON-EIGHTEEN

A YELLOW BIRD STARTS A NEW COACHING JOURNEY FOR A DIFFERENT KIND OF REASON

TRINITY CHRISIAN SCHOOLS

We moved to Lubbock and bought our tenth house. Jeany received a teaching position at Estacado High School in the English department as a lead teacher **TEACHING** the State English exam. Soon, Jeany had more than her share of work, going to work at 7:00 a.m. and coming home around 6:00 p.m. She would come home and go straight to bed for a nap, and then get up around 8:00 p.m. She finally had some down time from 8:00 p.m. to 10:00 p.m. Needless to say, she was working a lot harder than I was. It was not difficult for me in terms of coaching and being committed to a school. I really enjoyed the athletes at Trinity because they were so hungry for a coach to really coach them, or at least that is what they thought. Trinity didn't have an athletic period, so I started one at 7:00 a.m. - 8:00 a.m. in the morning. I was surprised at how everyone reacted, and soon we were filling the outdoor courts at 7:00 a.m. in the morning. The only thing I didn't count on was the time change, where you have more daylight in the afternoon and less in the morning. But by that time, we could start afternoon practices by the rules set forward by the Texas Association of Parochial Private Schools, called TAPPS. I couldn't decide whether dealing with parents or players was worse from the standpoint of understanding the difference between playing to participate and playing to win. Of course, the faculty had no clue, and I found that to be normal because the principal didn't even know when we had an athletic contest. I was an outsider, for sure, and often felt like I was beating my head up against a wall. But I wasn't discouraged at all because I could see potential in everyone, including the entire group at Trinity Christian Schools. The school was more about a family atmosphere, and because of that, I knew I had a chance at changing attitudes about athletics. Everything was going as expected when, late one night, Jeany and I received a phone call from a friend of Marcy's, telling us that Marcy had made a suicidal attempt on her life. She said that Marcy was in a special hospital ward at West Texas State University, located in Canyon, Texas. I can't even begin to tell you how guilty we both felt because we didn't pick up on the signs of her being depressed. It was a shock for us, and we really just didn't understand what was going on. When she was released from the hospital ward, she was in no shape to continue school at West Texas State University, so she came home with us and dropped out of school. Little did we know at that time, but our lives would never be the same. Soon we started looking for medical help. I really got upset with the so-called medical doctors and psychiatry in general. They charge a huge fee that is not close to being fair for someone that is mentally

CHAPTER NINE

COACHING LESSON-ONE
IT TAKES A FAMILY TO CHANGE AN ATTITUDE
TRINITY SCHOOLS

Coach Mayberry learned a huge lesson trying to teach private school administrators, teachers, parents, and players the difference between playing to win and playing to participate. It takes a family to change, and that is what it took for Trinity to understand that playing to win has more benefits than playing to participate. Trinity wanted to change but when it came time to do what was necessary to change, often they would rebel against the change. That is normal and is part of change. Don't get discouraged but stay the course and be focused. Remember, you can't do it by yourself, but together you can get the job done.

COACHING LESSON-TWO
ARE YOU USING THE TALENT GOD GAVE YOU?

Coach Mayberry is hit head on by a sermon at church about following God's plan. The bottom line is that most coaches feel they were called to coach. If you feel that way, then stick with his calling but listen to what he is saying and give back more than you take. Personally, I give

God all the credit for my success because I know it to be true. Success followed me, and the reason is that I had good athletes, so to this day I believe he is the one that directed my journey. I felt like he wanted me to start another journey, so I did, and now I know why, but I didn't at the time. After retirement, I coached for nineteen more years, and I was able to make a difference in the lives of young people, including my youngest daughter. If you feel you are called to coach, then follow that calling and give back all the good you can.

COACHING LESSON-THREE
JOIN THE FRATERNITY FOR COACHES THAT BENEFIT COACHES

One of the major advantages of coaching is developing friendships in the coaching fraternity. The coaching fraternity is one of a kind, but to be part of it, you must reach out to other coaches as friends. The more you reach out, the more friendships you develop. THE BOND YOU MAKE WITH COACHES LASTS A LIFE TIME. That is why it is a special profession.

COACHING LESSON-FOUR
THERE ARE MANY WAYS TO COACH-LEARN THAT EARLY AND YOU WILL BE A BETTER COACH
ROBERT LEE HIGH SCHOOL   1A

Coach Mayberry works with a football coach that works at football like no other football coach he has been exposed to. He soon learns that his ways of coaching were just as good as the ways Coach Mayberry understood. There is no certain way to coach but the most successful coach finds ways to coach that fit their personality. Just because they are different doesn't mean they can't coach.

COACHING LESSON-FIVE
ONE OF THE JOYS OF COACHING IS STAYING IN TOUCH WITH YOUR EX PLAYERS AND FOLLOWING THEIR SUCCESS
OZONA HIGH SCHOOL   2A

When it comes down to life, it is a small world, and you never know when someone from your past will appear, especially in the coaching world. Steve Taylor coached three young guys, that I coached in Hereford, Texas. All went into coaching and they were successful. How you treat your players is the most important issue in coaching. You will never know when the tables will turn and you will need their help again. This was a classic example because I didn't know Steve Taylor and he didn't know me, but we had heard about each other from those guys. That is why when we first met, we hit it off right away. We both had a trust factor already built in by those young men.

COACHING LESSON-SIX
ONE GREAT FACT ABOUT COACHING, WHEN YOU DO THE JOB AND DO IT WELL, GOOD THINGS HAPPEN
HOWARD JUNIOR COLLEGE   D1

By fate, Coach Mayberry stops at a Dairy Queen in Big Spring, Texas to get something to eat. When he gets inside, he runs into a long-time coaching friend named Tommy Collins. Coach Collins is now the Athletic Director at Howard College, located in Big Spring, Texas. Tommy was having a meeting with some administrators at Howard and

Coach Mayberry knew who they were. After all, he spent fourteen years coaching in the Western Junior College Conference, going to meetings that they attended. Coach Mayberry found out that they were looking for a women's basketball coach and he offered his services. Soon he was hired. Coaching is one of the few professions where almost everyone from the outside has an opinion on your ability to coach. If you do the job, they will know, and you don't have to advertise your abilities. Administrators that are in the hiring position should keep their ears and eyes open concerning prospective coaches. Coach Mayberry had put together a record of wins and losses in the Western Junior College conference that very few could match, and he had been directly involved in taking three programs that were at the bottom and putting them at the top. It was a no-brainer to hire him at Howard College. What all coaches must understand is that if they do a good job, it is not going unnoticed because someone is paying attention.

COACHING LESSON-SEVEN

THE DIFFERENCE BETWEEN COACHING MEN AND WOMEN? HOWARD COLLEGE   D1

Coach Mayberry has had the unique opportunity of coaching high school boys, high school girls, college men and college women. He has been asked many times what the difference is between coaching the two genders. Many coaches think they can jump from one gender to the other without missing a beat. I have even heard some coaches' claim that there is no difference because it is just basketball. I will tell you right now that the two are different and who you hire to coach which gender is most important. It takes a certain type of personality to coach girls/women and a certain type of personality to coach boys/men. My personality is more suited for boys and men. I had to learn that the hard way, and it's not like I can't, but I found that my personality is better suited to coaching the male gender. To figure out which gender you fit best, just take your worst personality traits and ask if they fit the girl better or the boy better.

COACHING LESSON-SEVEN
DOES ANYONE APPRECIATE THE JOB YOU ARE DOING?
WELLMAN UNION HIGH SCHOO   1A

Coach Mayberry's team at Wellman Union didn't make the playoffs, but they did have a winning season. Coach Mayberry will tell you today that he did the very best job of coaching that he has ever done that year, but there were no playoffs, no awards, nothing at all to hang your hat on. That is coaching and only a coach can understand. Those outside your arena are always more alert to what is going on in your arena than most people inside your arena. Often times a coach feels that no one appreciates the job they are doing and inside your arena, that is most likely close to being right. But outside your arena, everyone knows what is going on because it is the nature of the beast.

COACHING LESSON-EIGHT
THE DIFFERENCE BETWEEN COACHING BASKETBALL IN TEXAS AND NEW MEXICO
ST. MICHAELS HIGH SCHOOL   3A

Coach Mayberry couldn't get over the differences between coaching basketball in Texas and New Mexico. Many times, since he has learned the differences, he often says that if he had known what he knows now, he would have started his coaching career in New Mexico. Too him, the biggest difference is that in New Mexico, the coaching administration works at keeping sports from overlapping which gives the athlete a chance to play more sports.

COACHING LESSON-NINE
WHAT REALLY SEPARATES A REAL LEADER?
ST. MICHAELS HIGH SCHOOL   3A

Coach Mayberry meets two people that will remain two of his favorite administrators for the rest of his life. One was the Athletic Director and the other was the Physical Education Chairperson. Both were outstanding administrators because they both took care of student and teacher needs, but remained fair and always tough. But the most important issue was that they made you feel important.

COACHING LESSON-TEN
IF YOU WANT SUPPORT FOR YOUR ATHLETIC PROGRAM, YOU MUST SUPPORT ALL THE ATHLETIC PROGAMS
ST. MICHAELS HIGH SCHOOL   3A

Coach Mayberry was asked by the football coach if he would do a big favor for him. He asked Coach Mayberry not to badmouth his football program. Professional behavior works both ways for any teacher, coach, or administrator. If you want support, you need to give support. The best thing you can do for everyone concerned within your school is to support all programs at the school in a positive way. When you do just that, you will gain support in return many times over what you gave.

COACHING LESSON-ELEVEN
NEVER ASSUME ANYTHING IS THE ARENA OF COACHING ST. MICHAELS HIGH SCHOOL   3A
ST. MICHAELS HIGH SCHOOL   3A

Coach Mayberry learns after the season is over that the same players that he had trouble with during the year were the same guys that the previous coach had trouble with. In the previous coach's resignation letter, he stated that he just couldn't coach them and that was why he was resigning. Coach Mayberry assumed too much and paid the price. A coach must know ahead of time about everything that happened the year before, regardless of who is telling the story. Perception is everything, and a coach with enough experience can read through perception that is biased. But when enough events occur to back up what he heard, then that gives a coach a point of perception that is important in coaching. The more knowledge you have of your players, the better you can coach them and the better you can understand their behavior. Leadership is the root of all that is good or evil. Every team usually has both going for them, but what decides the direction a team takes depends on which one the team feeds off the most.

COACHING LESSON-TWELVE
IT IS ALMOST IMPOSSIBLE FOR A ATHLETE TO UNDERSTAND SOMETHINGS THAT THEY CAN'T SEE
ST. MICHALELS HIGH SCHOOL   3A

Coach Mayberry went to work making players better by using his off-season program. The results were excellent, but the main difference was taking them to watch the Metro State workout. With the help of my assistant coaches, we took our players to watch the Metro State workout. I want the players to play hard. I want my assistant coaches to coach hard, and sometimes that concept is very difficult for everyone to understand. If there is no one on your team that plays hard, it is impossible for them to understand. I explained that concept to all the players before we went to watch Metro State workout because they would demonstrate what I meant by playing hard. It was awesome, and no one was disappointed. For the first time, most of the players understood what I wanted. Now all we had to do was back that up with intensity ourselves and the rest would follow. The results were in the pudding. We won twenty-seven games that summer with only six losses. They followed that up with a district championship, a regional championship, and then qualified for the state championship. It was a complete turn-around. Playing hard is the key to playing well. Talent does not replace playing hard—nothing does.

COACHING LESSON-THIRTEEN
WHAT COMES AROUND GOES AROUND
TEXAS TECH UNIVERSITY NCAA   D1

Coach Mayberry needed a part-time position and Texas Tech had one. Because of his past relationship with the assistant athletic director and the athletic director, his chances for getting the position were excellent. There is an old saying that goes, "What goes around comes around," and this situation certainly fits that saying. Regardless of who you are, your past will come back to you in some shape or form. Be humble and professional in whatever you do

COACHING LESSON-FOURTEEN
<u>YOU WANT TO KNOW WHY YOUR TEAMS IN-WHY THEY LOSE-WATCH YOUR PRACTICE</u>
TRINITY CHRISTIAN SCHOOLS

Coach Mayberry hadn't been back to Trinity Christian since 1995. However, Coach Mayberry had stayed in touch by reading the sports page. He was surprised because Trinity was beating schools in BOYS AND GIRLS basketball that they never had before. He decided to find out what was going on, so he went to Trinity to visit with the Athletic Director. But the minute he walked into the **TRINITY GYM** he knew why they were winning because of the sounds of the workout going on when he entered the gym. Tennis shoes were talking loud and clear with each player's footwork. Constant verbal exchange between players was loud and body movement could be heard the minute he walked into the gym. In high school, this behavior is a sure sign that you are around a team that doesn't expect to be a win some, lose some team. However, in college, that isn't always true. Often, players pace themselves in workouts, never extending their effort to the point of really playing hard. Because of their athletic ability, they can fool you into thinking they are playing hard. The only ones that are getting cheated are themselves and the coach.

CHAPTER TEN

COACHING LESSON-ONE

A YELLOW BIRD BECOMES AN OLD YELLOW BIRD BUT HIS PASSION FOR COACHING NEVER ENDS

KIRKLAND CENTRAL HIGH SCHOOL   4A

Kirkland, New Mexico is located about ten miles on the west side of Farmington, New Mexico. Kirkland is about seventy miles east of the famous Four Corner Monument. That happens to be the only place in the United States where four states intersect at one point: Arizona, New Mexico, Utah, and Colorado. The Navajo Nation, which is one of the largest tribal nations in the world. It covers 27, 425 square miles around the city of Kirkland, New Mexico. The dominant racial makeup is Native American. The Athletic Director at Kirkland Central was direct and right to the point. He said that they expected to win a state championship in girls' basketball. He said that if that scared me, then don't consider taking this position. I had never had anyone be that direct in my life, but I really liked it. Then he told me the complete story about the girls' basketball program. It was a sad deal for everyone concerned, and he was just trying to make the best of a bad situation. Kirkland Central girls' basketball was a powerhouse basketball program, winning sixteen state championships. Banners are located in the gym, and it was clear that they had a lot of pride in the program. Last year the girls faltered with a poor record and didn't even make the playoffs. That just didn't happen at Kirkland Central. Two weeks into the current school year, the girls' basketball coach was fired. Not only did they fire him, but they fired all the assistant coaches, leaving no one to coach the team. It turned ugly, and because of the way everything was handled, no one trusted anyone. What made it worse for whoever followed in this situation was the fact that the fired coach was staying on board as a teacher and his daughter was a key player returning to the team. Coaching girls' basketball was a total nightmare. From the day I started, we had so many distractions, conflicts, and issues that I could understand why no one wanted this job. It started when I tried to hire my assistant coaches for the coming season. The superintendent sent word that I could hire anyone I wanted, including the old coaches that were fired. Of course, the best prospects for the jobs were the old coaches, so when I recommended hiring two of them, she said no. Then later, she came back and said yes to one of them. So, I hired one man who was back from last year and two women who were new in some way but not totally new. My main assistant coach was an assistant coach that was fired, so it shocked me when I found out he knew his stuff. He was a good coach and a good person. I found out that the reason he didn't get the job was because someone started a rumor that he was having an affair with one of the players.

COACHING LESSON-TWO

HOW TO MAKE THE BEST OF A TERRIBLE JOB IN COACHING KIRKLAND CENTRAL HIGH SCHOOL   4A

Coach Mayberry took over a basketball program that had so many problems and distractions that he resigned before the season started. From the first day, he had administrative problems, cultural problems, assistant coach problems, player chemistry problems, injury problems, school board problems, discipline problems, and personal problems. It was a nightmare, and he was supposed to win the state championship. He put a chip on his shoulder and attacked each problem one at a time without fear of failure. His resignation gave him the freedom to not worry about who he made mad or who didn't like what he was doing, and because of that, he had success. Solving problems is not going to happen by being a "good ole boy".

COACHING LESSON-THREE
THINK TWICE BEFORE YOU OPEN YOUR MOUTH WHEN YOU ARE IN THE SPOTLIGHT
KIRKLAND CENTRAL HIGH SCHOOL   4A

Regardless of the problems, Coach Mayberry guided the team of girls at Kirkland Central to the State Championship on the 4A level of play in New Mexico. In order to get to the state championship Kirkland Central defeated the #1 team in New Mexico. Coach Mayberry was quoted by the Roswell Newspaper in a misprint that the semi-final game was full of nick-picking fouls called by the basketball officials. Coach Mayberry never said that but instead was baited by a mad newspaper man from Roswell, New Mexico because he thought his team got beat because of a nick-picking foul. Kirtland Central upset Roswell in the semi-finals of the state tournament on a last-second foul by Roswell. The newspaper guy from Roswell claimed that the foul shouldn't have been called. He called it a nick-picking foul. Coach Mayberry opened his mouth and said, "Well, if that is the case, then all the fouls were nick-picking fouls." Coach Mayberry defended the officials but that was never mentioned in the newspaper. Instead, the paper came out saying

Coach Mayberry said all the fouls in the game were nick-picking. Then, during the **championship game, several fouls were called on Kirtland Central that Coach Mayberry didn't see. Finally, Coach Mayberry challenged one of the basketball officials, and the official said, "Coach, I guess that is one of those nick-picking fouls."** Sometimes we are misunderstood, especially when a coach defends his team because they feel their team is being treated differently by officials from another team they are playing. After watching game film, 95% of the time, the coach will be wrong. But this Coach Mayberry knew in a second that he had put his team in a bad spotlight by his comments to a sports reporter. What made it worse was that Coach Mayberry knew his comments were misprinted in order for the sports writer to justify their team getting beat. Then when an official that was calling the championship game made his comment back to him about nick-picking fouls, Coach Mayberry knew the game was over and it was going to be his fault. The lesson is simple. When someone is baiting you for a comment, be very careful what you say because it can be used against you in the heat of the battle. What made all of this so unfair is that Coach Mayberry didn't even have a negative attitude about the officiating at any point during the playoffs, but the Roswell sports editor did, and he used Coach Mayberry to get his point over to the public.

COACHING LESSON-FOUR
FIFTH SEASON OF PARTICIPATION
TRINITY CHRISTIAN SCHOOLS

COACH MAYBERRY learned that in the TAPPS [Texas Association of Private Schools] that you could coach and workout in the summer. Coach Mayberry raised the standards for workouts and commitment toward the program at Trinity Christian. They worked out four times a week during the summer and played forty games. The results were great in terms of improvement for all the players involved, but there were problems. Commitment and work are necessary if change is to occur, but always understand that there is a cost involved, and sometimes that cost is high.

COACHING LESSON-FIVE
ENVIRONMENT HAS A STRONG INFLUENCE ON THE WAY OFFICIALS OFFICATE A BASKETBALL GAME
TRINITY CHRISTIAN SCHOOLS

Coach Mayberry had learned early in his coaching career how to coach the "Four Corner Offense" by Dean Smith. He had coached this offense in states such as Texas, New Mexico, Kansas, Colorado, and Oklahoma. His experience taught him that officials have a tendency to think differently when you use the four-corner offense. The major thought process when a team uses the four -corner offense is that they are stalling. When that thought process kicks in, officials usually start looking for calls instead of letting it happen. It is human nature, and in those states listed, that was the case most of the time. But in North Carolina, that was not the case because officials had a great amount of respect for the four- corner offense and just continued to call the game the way they normally call a game. People in North Carolina understood that the four- corner offense was just that-it was an offense just like any offense and not just a stall. Because of that attitude, officials didn't start anticipating calls before it happened. Coach Mayberry took his girls team at Trinity to a large Women's basketball tournament in North Carolina. There were over 200 teams involved playing at different levels of play. Trinity entered the largest division that they had. Most all the teams were better and bigger than Trinity. An example would be that Trinity had 185 students in their school. There was not a school that had under 1000 student in the tournament. Coach Mayberry taught his girls the four- corner offense because he knew that they would need the offense in this tournament. Long story short, Trinity won the tournament. There was not a team that Trinity played that Trinity was better or more talented. The officials knew the offense and called the game in an awesome way. My point is that officials in different states call a little differently because of the background experience that carries over from the games they officiate. An example would be New Mexico officials. Often, New Mexico officials do a better job of calling a game that is up and down at a fast pace with the defense applying full court pressure. The reason is that that is what they see a great deal of the time. On the other hand, New Mexico officials have a hard time calling a game where a big player plays who is athletic with skills. The reason is that they seldom experience that kind of play in New Mexico, but in Texas it occurs a lot in the large cities. In Kansas, officials usually let the players play defense in a more aggressive style of play than in many states. That is because Kansas University is known for its aggressive style of play on the defensive end of basketball. Because of that, many high schools attempt to duplicate how Kansas University plays defense and then officials soon learn how to officiate that type of game. Texas is such a large state that you can find different styles of officiating depending mostly on the talent pool of athletes in certain areas of the state. Officials learn to call a high-quality game involving athletes in the southern part of Texas because that part of Texas usually has outstanding athletes playing basketball. Then if you jump into the West Texas and the Panhandle areas, you will find fewer athletes and fewer officials developing a style to fit into that group of athletes.

COACHING LESSON-SIX
LEADERS WORK BEST WHEN THEY COVER FOR EACH OTHER WEAKNESS AND STRENGTHS
ALL SAINTS SCHOOLS

Coach Mayberry is really impressed with the administrators at All Saints Middle School. Again, the main principle involved with good administration is that the administrators complement each other. That was the case at All Saints because the Head Master and the Assistant Head Master worked together for the benefit of all the students. They supported each other in personality and attitude, and they complimented each other, making the school a strong school. Where one was weak, the other was strong, and vice versa. They were a team, and together they were way above the normal administrator.

COACHING LESSON-SEVEN
IF YOU WANT CHANGE-IT MUST START WITH YOU-THEN YOU MUST LEAD AND BE PATIENT
ALL SAINTS SCHOOLS

Coach Mayberry is attempting to change behavior and attitudes concerning participation and winning at All Saints Middle School. I have been asked over and over what the key is to creating a change in attitude towards athletics. I can tell you in one sentence that it takes a family to change attitudes. What I mean is you by yourself can't do it, but with the help of many different kinds of people, it can be done. Change creates problems, and someone has to deal with those problems. The person that deals with the problems needs to be on your side or it can't be done. That is why I say family, because it takes all involved for change to be effective. But your attitude about work and getting along with all concerned is a must if any change has a chance for success. You must demonstrate an unselfish attitude, a strong work ethic, and a commitment to all programs in the school if you want a family attitude

COACHING LESSON-EIGHT

A GOOD MENTOR KNOWS WHEN IT IS TIME TO STEP UP TO THE PLATE LUBBOCK CHRISTIAN UNIVERSITY
NAIA   D1

Coach Mayberry is excited because one of his favorite coaches was selected to be a college coach. Coach Mayberry had mentored Todd Duncan for many years, and now he was taking a huge step in the coaching business. Coach Mayberry knew that this young man thought he knew what he was getting into, but Coach Mayberry knew he really didn't know. So, Coach Mayberry stepped up to the plate and offered his services. Every coach thinks they know what they are getting into when they change jobs. A coach wouldn't change if they didn't think they didn't know what they were getting into, but the truth is that no job is exactly what you thought it was going to be. Going from high school to college is the biggest jump a coach can make because everything is different. All high school coaches think they can do it, but once they get into the job, they realize that they really didn't understand what they were getting into. That is when a mentor is needed.

COACHING LESSON-NINE
WORK EITHIC IS SOMETHING THAT A COACH CAN NOT FAKE NAIA D1

Coach Mayberry gave advice left and right, but Todd Duncan was still trying to figure out the college game himself, so most of his advice went in one ear and out the other. However, Todd did listen to Coach Mayberry about one issue. Coach Mayberry told Todd that hiring an assistant coach in college is very critical. One characteristic that a college coach must have, is a great work ethic. **In college, your job is never over. It goes twenty-four hours a day and extends for three hundred sixty-five days a year. Many high school coaches are not ready for that issue. Coach Duncan hit the jackpot when he hired Jason Imes. What Coach Mayberry was worried about was Todd finding a person with the same kind of work ethic as Coach Duncan had. Coach Mayberry knew that Todd had an excellent work ethic and it bothered him because it is hard to find someone with that kind of work ethic. When he hired Jason Imes, Coach Duncan hit the jackpot.** Now they had to figure it out themselves in two different ways. Coach Duncan was coming from high school to NAIA D1 college basketball. That is a huge adjustment, and likewise, Coach Times was coming from Division One big time basketball to NAIA D1 college basketball. The difference between the two is like night and day. It may seem odd, but that was going to be a huge adjustment. Both were going to have to learn to adjust, and only time and experience could teach them what they had to learn.

COACHING LESSON-NINE
THERE IS AN OLD SAYING BUT IT IS STILL TRUE-EVERYTHING STARTS IN THE MIDDLE SCHOOL
CARLSBAD SCHOOLS   5A

You need to be involved/player development is critical. Coach Mayberry offers his service as the head basketball coach of Carlsbad, New Mexico. The eighth-grade class coming up is very talented and most likely the best ever in the history of Carlsbad. The Head Coach at Carlsbad hires Coach Mayberry to make a difference in their basketball future because, at this point in time, they were headed in the wrong direction. Everything negative and positive starts in middle school training. It can go either way, regardless of talent level. Coaches need to be alert and pay attention to the young players coming up, keeping close tabs on their talent, attitude, and work ethic. It starts at the middle school, and that is where it can be taught. If you wait until high school, most of the time it is too late. If you want to succeed, get involved in your middle school.

COACHING LESSON-TEN
IT'S NEVER TOO LATE TO LEARN-IT IS FUN AND ENJOYABLE TRINITY CHRISTIAN SCHOOLS

Coach Mayberry attempts to mentor Greg Ammons but ends up getting mentored by Greg. Coach Mayberry found Greg to be a special kind of coach and he enjoyed being around him and watching his teams play. If you read any paragraph in this book, please read this paragraph because what Greg does in the coaching world is needed and can be learned. He has the ability to give a player grace better than any coach I have ever been around. The minute they make a mistake, they are forgiven, and most importantly, they know it. That is a powerful tool in coaching. Coach Ammons is good about developing aggressive behavior from a fear of failure. He seldom overcoaches a player and always allows a player to be a player. He is not afraid to ask for help, but he is very selective in whom he asks. But what really impressed me the most about his coaching was how he could communicate with his players' parents. He did it in a way that they understood him, even if they didn't like what he said. Greg isn't perfect; he does have weaknesses just like all coaches, but he is a very good coach.

COACHING LESSON-ELEVEN

IT TAKES TWO TO TANGO

LUBBOCK CHRITIAN UNIVERSITY NAIA   D1

Coach Mayberry was impressed with the player his grandson had become while working under the direction of Todd Duncan and Jason Imes of Lubbock Christian University. Marcus Arrington, who is coach Mayberry's grandson, did a complete turnaround in terms of improvement from being a high school player to a college player. Everyone thinks the results are common, but the truth is that the results are not common. It takes two to tango, and nothing could be more the truth when it comes to athletic players getting better by being coached to become better. The coach is no better than the players' attitude towards getting better, and the players' attitude towards getting better is no better than the coach. When they are both on the same page, it works, but only if they are both on the same page.

Basketball coaching record [Two runners- up and one semi-final state championship] finished 5th at the National Junior College Tournament

High School boys and girls coaching record:
WON 422 LOST 160

College/Semi Pro Men's and Women's coaching record:
WON 486 LOST 167

Head coaching record:
WON 908 LOST 327

Middle School, Junior Varsity, Assistant coaching record:
WON 186 LOST 70

Total basketball coaching record:
WON 1094 LOST 396

Football coaching record:
[Two state championships and one- runner up state championship]
Assistant High School Coaching record: WON 105 LOST 25
Junior Varsity coaching record: WON 25 LOST 12
Total football coaching record: WON 142 LOST 43

Golf coaching record High School boys golf Class "A"
Texas State Championship
Women' College Golf Runner up National Championship

www.ingramcontent.com/pod-product-compliance
Lightning Source LLC
Chambersburg PA
CBHW060359080526
44583CB00012B/386